Red Clay Girl

A Memoir

EMILIE SPAULDING

Red Clay Girl
Copyright © 2016 by Emilie Spaulding

Photo credits: Front cover photo, Charlotte Frye; Back Cover photo, Jim
Cerny; Family photos – Albert Lorenzo Smith; Cable TV photos, Eric
Bergman; Emilie engagement photo, Jay T. Winburn.

Published by Piscataqua Press
An imprint of RiverRun Bookstore
142 Fleet Street | Portsmouth, NH | 03801
www.riverrunbookstore.com
www.piscataquapress.com

ISBN: 978-1-944393-16-8

First Edition
Printed in the United States of America

Dedication

To my mother, Esther Bubolz Smith, for
making me want to stand in the light and be
somebody

To my father, Albert Lorenzo Smith,
for loving me unconditionally

To my husband Dick, for his love, ideas, and
steadfastness

To our children, Amy Caroline, Susan
Pearson, and Kristiana Trow, for giving me
support without measure

To our sons-in-law, Bill, Joe, and Greg, and
our grandchildren, Will, Nick, Isabelle, and
Trow, for being just right.

To all, forgive me the times I've said,
"Not now, I'm writing."

TABLE OF CONTENTS

It takes courage
to grow up and become
who you really are.

e.e. cummings

SATURDAY NIGHT IN GRIFFIN, GEORGIA

In Griffin, Georgia, where I was born, there were four things that were strong: sweet tea, our accents, hot sauce on barbeque, and people's opinion of your place in the pecking order.

On the top rung were the upper-class families. They lived in houses that had music rooms where marble statues seemed to listen from the corners; their libraries were full of leather-bound books. Their closets were filled with shoes, soft as butter and kept in shape with wooden stretchers, resting under custom-made clothes. Maids in black uniforms with white chiffon aprons answered the front doors.

Next was the middle-class—business people,

clergy, teachers, artists, and scientists like my father. You could see them in church on Sunday; you knew they had chicken and biscuits for Sunday dinner at exactly 1:00 p.m. Their children kept the piano teacher busy and gave us all recitals to go to, where we could be proud of ourselves and each other.

At the bottom of the ladder were poor folks. They kept broken-down cars on cinder blocks in their side yards, flowers in tire planters up front, and the upholstered seats from pickup trucks nestled on their porches. But the best thing about their yards were the dazzling displays of colored bottles hung upside down on branches of leafless trees, so the sun shone through projecting colors that danced on the ground. Moms would never let us make a bottle tree at our house because she thought they were lowbrow. I thought they were works of art.

Living on the other side of the railroad tracks with their own neighborhoods, schools, and churches were the colored people. Those with very dark skin were at the bottom, just above were people with lighter skin, and the coloreds who could pass for white held a spot at the top, which all seemed so unfair.

One of our family's favorite outings in the mid-1940s was going downtown on Saturday night. It was the only day of the week when colored people, poor white folks, and the middle class went into town at the same time. Everyone was there except the richest folks, who hung out at the country club or retreated to mountain cabins.

Before we could go, Daddy always said, "Do your jobs first." So my sister Janet and I would sit on the screened porch shucking corn and stringing green beans as fast as we could. I still remember the feel of field peas. Their long, slimy pods felt wet like a frog's skin as we slid our fingers down the hulls to get the speckled peas to fall into the enameled pan.

Saturday was also the day we helped with the wash. I thought it was dreamy to hear the swish of the agitator twisting back and forth in the round open-topped washing machine. Soapy steam wafted into our faces. When the machine stopped, I'd untangle the clothes and feed them through wringers. The two rubber rollers would separate a bit to let the bulky clothes pass, at the same time squeezing out the water. If I were daydreaming, as I often was, my arm would get stuck between the rollers. That pinched it red. "Come quick," I'd yell up the basement stairs.

Once Daddy put a long string attached to the switch to turn off the electricity. If my arm started to get caught, all I had to do was pull the string. He thought that a lot easier than any attempt to stop me dreaming.

The washer did stop when I pulled the string, but my thoughts about leaving the south to travel to exotic places like Asia or Africa kept racing through my mind. Sometimes my dreams seemed so real that I once told my teacher I'd been to the country where tigers lived, though in reality I'd made a more modest journey to the Atlanta zoo.

When five o'clock on Saturday came around, the whole family would pile into our green Buick. We each had a given spot to sit in, no matter how short the trip. Alan would crawl into the middle back because he was the youngest and had to sit on the hump. Janet would take the right back window and I would take the left. Moms was the co-captain from the passenger seat. Daddy followed her instructions because he loved her, but there may have been a pinch of avoiding her displeasure.

One Saturday, Alan wanted to go to the train station. Since he was Moms' favorite, that was chosen as our first stop. As we neared, we saw black puffs of smoke. A steam engine came into view. Alan pumped his arm up and down until the engineer tooted the whistle, and the train squealed to a stop.

An employee with clothes as dusty as the train shoveled coal into the hopper.

Singing and swinging his shovel in rhythm to "Swing Low, Sweet Chariot," he put water into a funnel on top singing, *Comin' fo' to carry me home.* When he finished the job, we heard, *A band of angels coming after me,* and then he slowly walked back into the depot singing, *Comin' fo' to carry me home.*

I wanted to say Amen, brother, but Moms wouldn't have liked that.

Janet, Moms' second favorite, asked to look in the department store windows. "If I had one of those puffy

4

crinolines, Helen and I could swap off wearing it and boys would go wild over those sling-back shoes," she said. She could only dream, since our parents were frugal enough to wait until the stores closed before going into town.

We went into the drugstore, my choice, last. Everywhere you looked there were glass jars holding thermometers, powders, candy, and medicines. Nothing ever changed, but I liked the sameness. We sat at a marble counter with chrome stools and ordered ice cream in tall glasses. I always ordered vanilla, unless I was with friends who loved chocolate. Then I'd order chocolate to fit in, even though it tasted like dirt to me.

When we came out at dusk, four very dark men were bent under a spreading oak, bouncing dice off the shiny wall under the plate glass window of a pawn shop, passing a bottle in a paper bag among them.

"What're they saying?" I asked Daddy.

"That's called Geechee, Toots."

I wondered how we could all be from Griffin and speak different languages. Most of the people I knew sounded exactly as I did. Maybe this was like when outsiders had a hard time understanding me.

Our family's Saturday night routine being complete, we kids walked as slowly as possible back to the car parked near the Piggly Wiggly on the edge of town. We wanted to make the time last longer.

As we turned a corner I heard sharp voices pinging off the brick buildings like the dice we'd heard earlier, only louder.

"String him up!" They repeated it over and over. A few men had torches made out of sticks with rags lighted on top, the only thing that lit the moonless night. Daddy herded us three kids into the car.

"Lock the doors and don't open them for anyone, except me," he said sternly.

"Get down on the floor and pretend you're hiding," Moms said, getting in and pushing down the lock buttons. Red clay and pine needles stuck to the car rug where Janet, Alan, and I were smushed together. After what seemed to be a long time but probably wasn't, I wriggled up and looked out. I could see Daddy talking to someone at the edge of the crowd. Men swung their arms, tight fists pounded the air.

Daddy, who was Texan tall, jumped back into our car, locked his door, and without making the usual settling-in motions, started the motor and drove away. I held back sobs and wiped my eyes on my sleeve since I didn't have a hankie.

I looked all through the *Griffin Daily News* the next day. The front page featured a horse show that was being held the next weekend, a barbeque cook-off, and a notice about a meeting of the Masons, but not a word about what happened behind the Piggly Wiggly.

Daddy refused to talk about it, except to say, "It's okay, Toots. The sheriff came and sent the bad men home." Then Daddy said something I couldn't hear, under his breath.

Moms gave Daddy a look.

Other kids knew about the incident too. We whispered about it, mostly at the edge of the playground where we felt like we wouldn't be heard. If we said or did the wrong thing, would the bad men come for us and our families?

Now, my dreams turned bad. I saw shadowy figures lurking around corners. I heard mysterious footsteps following me as I ran into the woods next to our house.

Before this happened, I had thought there were three layers of people in our town. I learned better.

Like the six-layer cake I ate at Morrison's Cafeteria in Atlanta, there were probably at least that many layers of people in Griffin—not all of them feeling kindly toward each other.

In addition to the Ku Klux Klan, there were the lodges with secret handshakes and meetings, the Geechee who seemed loyal to their ancient culture, the merchants who owned movie theaters and enforced the strictest of rules, USDA Experiment Station scientists who focused on breeding only the fittest of plants, and bridge players who stayed in their close-knit social circles. There was even a plain ole mean boy at the edge of town who spun kittens around in an open umbrella.

Were there eddies of different ideas in every small town, swirling like waters in a pond, sometimes washing over each other and other times drowning out the rest?

For the next several Saturdays we didn't go into town, but stayed home and played Go Fish or Monopoly. Every card I laid down made sense, but the stirrings inside me didn't.

Mother and Daddy
Esther Emilie Bubolz was born in Wisconsin.
Albert Lorenzo Smith was born in Chickashaw,
Indian Territory – later Oklahoma. They met in
graduate school at the University of Wisconsin.

9

Janet Diane and Emilie Sandra-Lynn Smith at
509 E. College Street, Griffin, Georgia.

THUMPING A WATERMELON

"Toots," Moms said to me as she idled the car near the curb at the Piggly Wiggly, "run in and pick out a watermelon. Be sure it's ripe. When I cut it I don't want it pink, but red. And not gone by sugary. You do know how to thump a watermelon, don't you?"

"Yes, ma'am," I said.

Well, sort of, actually, not really. But I did know not to get into all that when Moms was in a hurry. I'd just ask someone who looked like they knew. That was easier than risking Mom's wrath.

"I'll be back," she said as she sped away.

The plate glass windows were plastered with handwritten specials: Twelve Corn—99 cents. Six Coca-Cola—99 cents. And Watermelon—99 cents.

Although I was eleven years old, my eyes were level with Moms. She was five feet tall in her stockings, which she rolled on elastic bands just below her knees. We were both thin. But she had black wavy hair and a turned-up nose like her Prussian grandparents. My hair was brown and straight, and I resembled my daddy's British ancestors.

The produce section was crowded and smelled like juicy ripe peaches. The okra looked green and hairy, but that didn't matter; everyone knew how good it was dipped in corn meal and fried in lard.

When I reached the melons, I started thumping them with my finger. The thumps were pitched too high. I knew I wanted one that sounded like a frog's deep croak at the bottom of the well.

A colored man approached, sweeping with a straw broom that made scritch-scratch noises on the pine floor. Maybe he could pick out the perfect melon for me. Then Moms would be pleased.

"Excuse me," I said to the man. "Would you please thump a watermelon for me? My mother is particular and I can't seem to find a good one. Besides, my finger is getting sore!" I smiled at him, my best I-need-a-favor smile.

He didn't say anything. He didn't look up. He moved to the back of the store. He swept what he'd already swept rather than sweeping where I was, which was littered with produce leaves.

Maybe he's hard of hearing, I thought. I followed and asked in a slightly louder voice, "Would you please thump a watermelon for me, sir?"

He turned and disappeared behind a tall display of Corn Flakes.

I asked a few customers if they could help, but they all shook their heads, saying things like, "Oh, my, I'm not good at that."

Moms would be back soon. I stood there in my short-sleeved shirt, denim shorts, and scuffed sandals, twisting my fingers. I'd been there so long that no one was left in the produce department. They had probably all gone home to fix lunch. Maybe they'd eaten lunch by now. I could imagine their fresh corn with dripping butter, melted in the heat of the sticky air, with plastic corn-shaped holders jabbed into the ends.

Just then, I heard a noise behind me. Turning quickly, I saw the sweeper pointing to a melon at the back of the bin.

"Do you want me to take this one?" I asked.

He didn't seem to hear me, but pointed a few more times to the same melon. I bent over and picked up the watermelon. Raising my head, I thanked him—or rather, thin air. No one was in sight.

I laid the watermelon down by the cash register and put a dollar bill on the counter. The clerk pushed two buttons of the scrolled-metal cash register, and "99 cents" popped up on white cards in the glass window. The drawer at the bottom popped open with a thud, hitting a pile of flyers. The clerk handed me a shiny penny.

"Goodness child, what took you so long?" Moms

said as I got back into the car.

"I'm pretty sure I got a perfect melon," I said, handing her the penny. Moms always insisted on our giving her the change. Not to do so was considered stealing.

That afternoon, neighbors and church friends at Moms' picnic raved about her fried chicken and biscuits, but what I heard loudest was, "This is the best watermelon I've had all summer."

"Toots picked it out for me this morning," Moms said.

I accepted her hard-to-come-by compliment, which wasn't mine to keep. But I couldn't risk getting the sweeper in trouble. Mom's friends might have raised both eyebrows and said, "Well, I declare," and repeated the story. Studying her guests closely, I didn't think any of them would have reported a colored man for talking to a young girl in shorts, but you never knew for sure.

Wilma said, "Toots, you'll just have to come to town with me whenever I need to buy a watermelon." She reached for another piece and smoothed down the tiny flowers and twisting vines that appeared to be climbing all over her dress.

"Yes, ma'am, I'd be happy to," I said, hoping she'd forget.

I went back to the Piggly Wiggly with Moms on other trips, but the watermelon picker was never there. I didn't find out why and hoped I hadn't gotten him into trouble.

Once during the holidays, I imagined in my eleven-year-old mind, that perhaps the people in the Cadillac with Detroit plates were his son's family on vacation from working at the GM plant up north. Maybe they were here to take my friend to the beach in Panama City, Florida, and then back to live with them in Michigan.

Regardless, I'll always remember his kindness and feel sad that I didn't see him again to say, *thank you.*

CAUGHT IN THE MIDDLE

On November 9, my three-year-old sister Janet was quoted as saying, "I wanted a doll for my birthday, but I got a baby sister instead." I was that baby that didn't have a name picked out yet. She must have gotten over it, because we became buddies. When I recently asked Janet to remind me of times we fought, she was silent so long I thought she'd gone deaf. Finally, she said, "I can't think of any."

Four years after I was born, little brother Alan appeared at Thanksgiving, and everything changed. He had green eyes the color of a perch's fin, blond ringlets, and Moms' turned-up nose. Strangers said he was as adorable as Shirley Temple. I, at four, thought he was cute too, especially when he laughed and showed his dimples.

Almost immediately, though, dark clouds began to rumble, and Moms disapproved of everything I did. As if a switch had been thrown, Moms' adoring light now shone on Alan instead of me. I turned from being a happy girl into a frowning one oozing sadness.

Of particular disappointment was the fact that Moms let Janet take tap dance lessons while I had to sit and watch, even though it was I who more than anything in the world wanted to dance with Fred Astaire. Secretly, I practiced the moves at home. Sensing the situation, the teacher said, "Come on stage with Janet and I'll teach you for free."

One Sunday, the whole family went to Lebanon, Georgia, a half-hour's ride away, to attend the only Lutheran church in the area. I pleaded to wait in the car and Moms agreed. During the service that seemed to go on for hours, I got out of the car and stepped into the stone-floored vestibule. Whenever the organ played, I practiced my tap moves, and then sat in a carved chair to wait for the next music. Shortly before the end of the service, our family came out of the church. Alan was still coloring pictures in his busy book. Moms had that stern look on her face. She turned to me and said, "Toots, they could hear you tap dancing to the music, even over our singing." We had to leave early and miss the coffee hour so no one would figure out that it was me causing all that commotion. We never went back again.

Daddy, perhaps because he understood my situation, began treating me as if I were the most special person in the world. Weekends we would walk in the woods. He taught me how to identify trees.

"Maple leaves look like the flag of Canada. Willow trees droop down as if they are weeping tears into nearby water."

We would look for arrowheads along the creek. Toward the end of any unsuccessful hunt, Daddy would point to a spot and say how promising it looked. Then I'd find a hand-chiseled piece of flint used years earlier by Indians hunting along the same streams. Later I realized those relics must have fallen out of Daddy's pocket.

Evenings, he would ask me about my day. When I walked with him at night after supper, I'd always stop and place my foot on the same dark spot on the sidewalk and whisper to whoever granted wishes, "Get me out of here so I can become someone important and do something special."

Just in case, I also practiced jumping off the chicken coop with an umbrella so I could run away and join the circus. Then they'd be sorry.

Toots, 2, the baby

Toots, 4, now in the middle

ROOSTER POEM

My first memory of being excited about writing was at six when watching our bantam rooster scratching for worms. With his red cock and iridescent black, orange, and bluish feathers, he strutted around our unfenced backyard. Hens clucked in a throaty symphony to keep their chicks close, or were they saying, *Rooster, notice me.*

I wore white sandals that needed a swipe of polish from that plastic container with the sponge on top. Those hand-me-down shoes slapped the hard ground as I raced inside, letting the screen door flap.

"Moms, do you have a pencil and paper? I need to write something down, it's important!"

"No child. Look by the phone. Maybe in the desk."

By the time I had searched and not found anything, the poem was evaporating from my head. So I said it over and over. It went like this:

Yellow forsythia blossoms
Dripping like a fountain
Skinny little girl
Sits cool underneath
Red-topped rooster
Struttin' his stuff,
G-l-o-r-y Be!

I didn't know then that Moms would be unavailable, and that writing would fill the crevices in my heart as I unspooled stories about the South, New York City, and beyond.

WHAT I DID ON MY SUMMER VACATION

At the Third Ward School in Griffin, Georgia, each morning, filled with patriotism and pride, we students and teachers rallied around the flagpole, put our hands on our hearts, and pledged allegiance to the flag of the U-ni-ted States of A-mer-i-ca. Then we sang "God Bless America." Every day topped up my patriotism and filled me with pride. Before the last note floated away on the hot Georgia air, *braaang*, the harsh-sounding go-to-class bell would bring us back to something less sure, teachers on a quest for perfect schoolwork, or at the very least perfect penmanship. Sometimes, as I walked inside, I could see the principal watching from his office window, his finger still resting on the bell.

On this first day of fourth grade, a new teacher swept into the classroom and hung her straw hat with a navy ribbon on the brass hook on the teacher's cupboard. The drawers below were filled with chalk, erasers, and writing tablets, and the shelves above with textbooks.

"Good morning, I am Miss Roberts." The chalk screeched as she wrote her name in script on the blackboard. Miss Roberts had blond hair and a big smile and took turns looking each of us in the eye, as if we were the only people in the world, or at least the state of Georgia, who mattered. I wondered what had happened to the crabby Miss Jones that Janet had warned me about. It was going to be a great year, I thought, until the teacher asked us to write about what we did on our summer vacations.

I didn't want to tell anyone about visiting my relatives in Texas. Maybe I could be sick the next day. That night, in perfect Palmer Method script, I wrote on white-lined paper, "What I Did on My Summer Vacation."

I thought about that summer's trip to visit my grandparents in Borger, Texas. We'd loaded the trunk of our Buick with our summer clothes, suntan lotion, and sunglasses, and stuffed the foot of the front passenger seat with maps of every state between Georgia and the Texas Panhandle, plus a basket of tomato and ham sandwiches lathered with Miracle Whip.

At Daddy's suggestion, Moms had brought the metal milk can filled with water. At every stop, even at a restaurant, we would fill it so we could quench the radiator's irregular thirst. At unexpected moments, steam was likely to curl out of every side of the hood.

We left the day after school let out. My six-foot two-inch dark-haired father squeezed himself in behind the wheel, eager to get started. Moms, in a tomato-red and white dress that matched the tomato sandwiches, sat in the passenger seat and gave directions.

"The next town is Meridian," she would say, or Tallulah, or Texarkana. "I think," Moms said, "the names of the towns are far more interesting than the highway numbers." I didn't want to admit that she was right. I sat on the white cotton shag seat cover between my parents, since I got car sick. I would have behind-the-scenes information if they whispered something while I was pretending to be asleep, even if it was the most uncomfortable seat in the car.

Janet perched at the right-hand back window, her new lipstick, "Cherries in the Snow," and her Girl Scout handbook in her lap. "I'm going to work on a travel badge," she said. No one else in the troop had that badge. Alan sprawled himself out on the left side of the backseat. He whistled or played his harmonica most of the way through Louisiana, Mississippi, and Arkansas. Janet and I threatened to kill him if he didn't stop. That is a southern expression of disgust, not a real promise.

Daddy had an irritating habit of pulling off on the shoulder of the road at every lyre-shaped metal historical marker. Frequently, it commemorated a battle that the South had actually won. At first we all got out of the car. Then just the kids got out. Pretty quickly, nobody but Daddy stirred. Leaving the motor running, he would start at the top and read down to, for instance, the last mention of the Cherokee Indians' Trail of Tears. The Cherokees were driven from their native lands in Georgia and the southeastern states to uncharted lands in the West, following this route. Then he would stick his left arm straight out of the window to signal we were continuing on our way, until the next darn marker.

The first two nights we camped on the uneven ground. It was quiet, just the hooting of an owl or a coyote's cry. On the third day we kids pleaded for a motel, where we put a quarter in the jiggle bed, took hot showers, and slept on white sheets that felt soft as chicken feathers.

At last, we pulled the Buick up in front of a modest white frame house. Early in the morning, Grandpa Lorenzo Smith, who was not particularly tall and was dressed in jeans, a T-shirt, and work boots, tapped on the car window. "Howdy. Come on in and have some breakfast."

Grandmother Molly Huggins Smith wore a thin cotton housedress and gave us all bear hugs. My grandparents laughed at almost anything. How much jollier they seemed than my Wisconsin grandparents, for whom everything had a serious purpose.

Lorenzo was a farmer, carpenter, freight hauler, and

road builder. Molly had adapted to being a frontier woman and instead of smoking cigarettes, to my dismay, she dipped snuff. She sat on the front porch in her rocker, laughing and telling family stories, stopping occasionally to spit juice into a blue Prince Albert tobacco can. I loved the stories. The snuff was disgusting.

If we got hungry between meals, Molly always had a big pot of white beans, onions, tomatoes, hot sauce, and a ham bone cooking on low on the back burner of the stove. We could just go and help ourselves. The first day the beans were so hard they could break your teeth. The second day the beans were softer. By the third day, they tasted heavenly.

One day, I found a small round ham bone with a hole in the middle nestled in my bowl of beans. It looked like an African queen's ring. An hour later, no one could get it off my finger—not with soap, twisting, or pulling. Finally, Daddy got the hacksaw and sawed it off.

Since the house was small, my father's sister, red-headed Juanita, gave us her bed and slept in a double hammock in the yard with her husband. You could hear crickets and their singing, "'Ain't nobody here but us chickens.'" And, probably to keep my grandmother Molly from complaining, they sang, "'Oh, oh, oh, me, oh, my Miss Molly, I'm in love with you.'" I think it was the chicken song that put me to sleep.

The scorching Texas sun beat down relentlessly,

day after day, so Molly put vinegar on my burns and a cool washcloth on my forehead. She talked about relatives who had moved around from state to state, looking for work. She called my dad "Sun." She told us it was spelled S-U-N. Daddy was the sun in my eyes too.

Back in class the second day of school, I read my story to Miss Roberts and the other fourth graders. I told them about our trip through different states, and how we'd stopped at Indian reservations and camped out. I mentioned how jolly our grandparents were, but I didn't mention the snuff or the cock fights or the oil pumps in people's front yards.

Putting myself in my classmates' shoes, if they had told me they had a grandmother who spit snuff juice into a Prince Albert can, I might have started looking at them funny and stopped being friends.

The thing is, in Texas I'd never laughed so much, sung so many old-timey songs, and felt so much love. I wondered if being poor came with having fun and having money came with being serious like my Wisconsin grandparents. I'm still not sure I know.

During WWII, at Fourth Ward School in Griffin, the Pledge of Allegiance and God Bless America rang out from around the flagpole every day, rain or shine. Toots in the middle, 9th from either side.

STUMBLING OVER THE BIBLE

Some summers, Moms and we three kids took two days and two trains to Appleton, Wisconsin, where her parents, Julius and Emilie Bubolz lived. A highlight (or lowlight in my case) was the Bible reading every night. Moms' oldest sister Lydia, the housekeeper, younger sisters Ethel and Gertrude, and several other relatives who lived nearby might drop in for the reading. Unlike Daddy's family's Texas nights, it was a somber half hour, followed by a prayer and a loud *amen.*

I was terrified of being the reader, although I loved to read, since I was afraid of making mistakes in this austere company. I tried to make myself invisible by scrunching down in a hidden spot with my eyes shut. That worked until the summer I was nine, when Julius chose me to read.

I started with a melodic psalm in a quivering voice. In the background was the ticking of the clocks my grandfather had collected, seeming to measure my progress. Younger relatives sat on oriental rugs with their knees crossed; aunts and uncles sat on stuffed chairs and fat sofas. I felt even skinnier than I usually did, and could sense my braids swinging and my braces clicking as I read.

A tickle started in my throat, a hiccup struggled to get out, and then I bit my finger as hard as I could so the pain would bring me back. Finally, I giggled until tears ran down my cheeks.

Janet elbowed me so she could take the Bible, and she continued reading the passage as if nothing had happened. I could always count on Janet.

My grandfather said in a kindly voice, "Toots, why don't you go to your room and reflect on the Bible passage?"

I ran up the stairs as fast as I could, jumped in bed, and pulled the handmade quilt with pink roses over my head. I decided I wouldn't get up in the morning and face people, just take the first train back to Alabama. That would be best.

Next morning, hungry as always, I crept downstairs for a piece of Aunt Lydia's fresh-baked kuchen before starting out. I was greeted by the whole family, early risers all, perhaps because they came from a line of dairy farmers who had always gotten up at 4:30 a.m.

for the morning milking.

No one mentioned the night before or seemed to care—not Moms, nor her sisters, not even Julius. So I stayed. They talked about how their cows had names such as Elsie, Polly, and Betsy, names painted on boards over their stalls. An uncle reported that cows gave more milk if the family talked to them. "It doesn't matter much what is said," he explained. Julius said that if you piped Bach or Beethoven into the barn, it triggered more milk. He didn't explain why, but I knew how important getting love was. Sitting around the table in the warm kitchen, I felt like I belonged with these handsome, congenial people. We were no longer strangers who saw each other once a year. And since I felt at home, I didn't stumble or giggle once.

Wisconsin relatives 1916, Front L to R: Gordon, Ethel, Julius (Dad),
Gertrude, Emilie (Ma), Lydia. Second row: Herbert, Louise, William,
Anna, George, Edmund, Julius Christian, Esther (our mother) and
Richard.

Aerial view of Bubolz dairy farm in Seymour, Wisconsin.
Birthplace of Esther (Moms)

AIR RAIDS

Neighborhood kids sat in a circle on our beige rug singing "Happy Birthday" as I blew out two candles on my cake and Janet blew out five candles on hers. We thought it was an ordinary week, until Daddy read to Moms from the *Atlanta Journal Constitution* that almost at the same time, Hitler's Brown shirts were breaking windows in Jewish-owned stores in Germany and taking men away on trains. "They call it Kristallnacht," he said.

"That means night of broken glass," Moms said. Of course, she understood German since her parents, Emilie and Julius, had come as small children with their families from Prussia to Wisconsin in the 1860s. Their parents were able in one year to become citizens, buy land, and farm the rich black soil.

As WWII approached, we were not allowed to tell anyone that Moms was of German descent. Southern neighbors didn't seem to care a whit about her nationality, only that she was a Yankee, which seemed to include anyone not from the South.

Having a Yankee in the family could have made things hard for us, but Daddy, who grew up in Texas, was embraced in Griffin and made up for any mistrust with his gentle, slow-talking ways. He was even designated an air raid warden, assigned to a nearby neighborhood. All other wardens were assigned elsewhere.

One night when the air-raid signal went off with a *woop–woop-woop* sounding in waves up and down the streets, Daddy rushed out to his post. Wardens made sure no lights shone from houses since enemy bomber pilots might see the light and use it as a target. I've wondered since, why German tacticians would schedule their bombers to go anywhere near our sleepy Southern town. Nevertheless, every time the air-raid siren sounded, Moms and we kids would turn out the lights, find our way to the back den with flashlights, and lower old blankets that had been tacked to the upper window frame. We'd read in the dim light until the sirens sounded the all clear. I liked to write poems in the dimly lit room.

One night when Daddy was out checking his designated neighborhood during a blackout, I heard men tramping around outside our house. They sounded so official, I wondered if they wore uniforms, high boots, or helmets like the German soldiers did in newsreels. I tiptoed over and lifted up a tiny corner of a blanket allowing a hint of light into the darkness. Disappointed that the men looked like ordinary daddies, I quickly flipped the corner back down. Later that night after Daddy got back, there were loud bangs on the front door. The neighborhood warden said gruffly, "We thought we saw a light coming from the back of your house tonight."

Daddy, without missing a beat, explained that we had put old blankets from the attic over the windows near the woods and one must have a moth hole in it. "We'll fix it first thing in the morning. Thanks for telling us," he said with appreciation in his voice.

"Y'all be sure you do that, then."

I don't think Daddy even looked for the moth hole. I'm certain he knew what had happened from the start, my always being curious. But he never mentioned it to me. And to this day, when I see a moth hole in anything, a wave of love washes over me.

Note: In 1946 we moved from Griffin, Georgia to Auburn, Alabama. Daddy taught cotton genetics to graduate students at Alabama Polytechnic Institute, now Auburn University, and he continued to work for the U.S. Department of Agriculture.

WWII Ration Book stamps would allow a shopper to buy rationed goods. The last line contains this sage advice, "If you don't need it, DON'T BUY IT." Bubble gum was unavailable.

MONTGOMERY BUS RIDE

"Toots, you need to get that orthodontist to fix your retainer."

It was broken since I'd sat on it by accident. The orthodontist was all the way in Montgomery, and we'd *always* driven, but this time Moms wanted me to take the bus alone since she had a substitute teaching job that day. I was twelve and the very thought of going to the capitol by myself made me bite my nails.

I didn't know exactly where his office was. All she'd given me was the address on the back of an old envelope.

"How do I know how to get there?" I asked.

"Just ask a stranger if you get lost."

Moms dropped me off at the bus station early the next morning. White paint hung down the outside of the bare wooden building in scattered peels. I went in and plunked down my money on the gritty ledge of the ticket agent's office, and sat down on one of the scuffed benches. The only decoration inside was a long strip of flypaper swinging from the ceiling fan. It was covered with petrified flies and dust. I went outside to wait, not wanting to get typhoid fever from touching anything inside.

Since it was still early, I walked down the right side of the building and saw a water fountain with a hand-lettered sign, *Whites Only!* I walked up and took long slurps of the icy cold water that squirted out and cooled me all the way down to my toes. That felt good on this hot, hot day.

Being curious, I wandered around to the back. *Colored Only!* said the hand-lettered sign hanging over a rusty, dented fountain. There was a piece of wadded gum on the rim that Noah must have left before he went to build the ark.

I wondered if the water tasted different, so I thought I'd try it. Wait, would someone run out and grab me, saying, "Don't you know you can't do that?" I tried the fountain anyway, but it didn't even work, so colored people who waited back here would have to stay thirsty, which seemed unfair.

When the Trailways bus pulled up front, the driver opened the door, which made a loud swooshing sound. The white passengers who had gathered climbed aboard and took all the front seats, back toward the middle section. I took my favorite spot, the right front, so I could watch everything.

When all the whites were seated, the bus circled around to the back of the building like a dog chasing his tail. There, colored people waited on benches, always outside. Mostly, they were cleaning women who carried totes full of rags and cleaning supplies in one hand, and empty sacks in the other, ready for the food and hand-me-down clothes the missus would give them. They struggled up the stairs with their parcels and headed straight to the back, seating themselves from the back toward the middle.

Soon, we bumped along the rough road, stopping to pick up more women who were waiting at gas stations. Colored stations sold anything you could think of: food, moonshine, scouring powder, seeds, peanuts, rope, and of course, gas. Without fail, at any country gas station, there would be wizened old men sleeping with their chairs tipped back against the building, wearing straw hats on their heads and faded overalls. Their hound dogs would be dozing at their feet.

Two hours after we'd started, we arrived at the bus station in Montgomery. White passengers got off first, heading toward work or other appointments. Then the colored women got off, going to clean in the big houses nearby. I started from the station to the orthodontist, stopping to show several people the address when I wasn't sure where to turn. At that time, Montgomery was as foreign to me as Paris.

When I got to the orthodontist, the receptionist said there was no appointment for me in the book. I told her I had come all the way from Auburn, by myself, to get my retainer fixed and it had taken hours.

"You can wait if you want, but I don't know what he will do," she said in a tight voice that sounded a bit like Moms when my brother brought snakes inside the house. Although I considered it, I couldn't leave and take the bus right back. Moms had given me instructions.

During the two hours I waited, I read the magazines about hunting, fishing, cooking, and my favorite, *The Saturday Evening Post*. When the orthodontist finally called me in, he said, "I don't care if you walked from Auburn, tell your mother it will be $50 to fix your retainer. I don't take charity cases," and he sent me out the door.

I hurried back to the station. It was bad enough that I was going to look like a buck-toothed rabbit for the rest of my life, but I didn't want to think what Moms would do if someone had to drive fifty-four miles each way to pick me up.

I was the last person to get on the bus before the huge door thumped shut. Since there were no empty seats in the white section up front, I sat down next to a colored woman in the middle. The white bus driver, whose name according to his badge was Charlie, twisted around and looked toward the back. "This will not do, there are ordinances," he said in a gruff voice while shaking his head.

"I don't mind sitting anywhere, really. Let's just go," I said.

But he walked back and said with gentle authority to the elderly woman sitting next to me, "Move on back."

She gathered her packages, rose with a sigh, and shuffled to the hard bench across the back—always the last seat taken. I thought everyone behind me would be aiming darts at the back of my head with their eyes, for having caused an old woman to move. I pretended, and then tried to sleep. When I wasn't feeling too nervous, I looked around, but no one was paying me any mind.

On the return trip, the driver made quick stops at the colored gas stations, but frequently he slowed and pulled off the road onto the red-clay shoulder at unscheduled stops. It was different from the trip in. A colored woman would make her way to the front, say good night to the driver, and get off where her driveway was so covered with bushes, you wouldn't know a house was back there.

Good, I thought, she'll be safer hidden away. No one can find her house to burn a cross in her front yard, as I'd seen done in a recent newsreel before a movie.

"Good night," the driver called to most by name.

The drop-off process was repeated over and over on Route 85, which we locals called the Montgomery Highway. Most didn't need to pull the cord to signal since the driver seemed to know their stops by heart.

"See you in the morning," they said to each other.

So, I asked if I could get off in Auburn at Samford Avenue, the first of two stoplights in town.

"Miss, I can only do it if there is a red light. There are ordinances when I reach the city limits."

I sank into my seat, feeling second class. But as we neared my intersection, the driver slowed almost to a stop, timing it so the light turned red just as we got there. He had planned it all along, it seemed. I was glad he had honored other riders as well as me, and felt that Charlie and the other riders and I were in this together. Sharing this secret made me more a part of what was going on, but I still regretted I couldn't share the Piggly Wiggly watermelon man's secret just like this.

As I passed the Texaco station on my half-mile walk home, I bought a bottle of Orange Crush and a small bag of salty peanuts. As I poured some of the nuts into the sweet drink and shook it up with my finger over the top, I could hear Moms' voice in my head floating over the waiting cars and the people pumping gas. "Salty nuts in a drink? That makes you look like po' trash, don't you go doing it."

I walked down the tree-lined sidewalk toward my house at 529 E. Samford Avenue, plopping the nuts into the bottle one by one. I loved those salty and sweet flavors, but my taste of freedom was even better.

Then I saw the red azalea blooming in our front yard, and I was home.

Three years later a colored woman, also riding a bus in Montgomery, refused to give up her seat while saying she was not just tired, but tired of giving in. A year-long boycott of buses followed, and in December of 1956, the US Supreme Court ruled that segregated buses were unconstitutional. Her name was Rosa Parks.

Rosa Parks, Montgomery Bus Boycott, 1955

SHOOTING FOR THE MOON

When I didn't have any chores, I practiced shooting baskets through a hoop nailed to the oak tree in our backyard. I got to be a pretty good shot from favorite locations I'd mark with an X in the red clay. It paid off one day after school when Gary said, "Wanna shoot some baskets?" "Sure," I said nonchalantly. "My house?"

Even at nine I recognized how handsome Gary was; he looked a bit like movie star Gary Cooper, whose picture I had pasted in a scrapbook. My Gary's brown wavy hair fell over his freckled forehead above a big toothy smile and dimples.

"Let's play PIG," I said when he arrived. "You go first."

The rules were if you made a shot from a particular line in the dirt and the other person couldn't make it, he or she was a P, then an I, and then a G. "You're a pig!" the winner would call out, and laugh. Having a goal made me try harder and was in good fun, I thought.

It turned out Gary wasn't a very good shot. We were laughing the first couple games. Then he had two or three PIGS and I had none, and it wasn't funny anymore. I thought maybe I should let him win.

I tried to miss a shot. Swish! Oops, it went in. I'll miss this next one then. But it always went through the hoop. Something was wrong. I couldn't make myself miss on purpose and let him beat me, even when I tried. And I liked him.

I was puzzled, because that wasn't what good church-going girls did—hurt other people's feelings on purpose. So I decided if I couldn't lose, I'd have to find a place where it was okay for girls to win, all the time. I would leave and find that place when I got older.

TWO TENNIS BALLS SHORT OF A SECOND SERVE

I thought of tennis and golf as being country-club sports. Maybe someday I'd belong to a club and play, but I didn't give it much thought. Then, one day when I was thirteen and walking home past the Auburn University courts, I saw an abandoned brown tennis ball lying in the clay behind the fence. To me, this was like finding a diamond in the dirt. I picked it up, crossed College Street, and bounced it all the way home.

When I went inside Daddy was sitting in the living room in his favorite chair, the one with the wide lima-bean-shaped arms on which could rest a book, magazine, or coffee.

"I found a tennis ball, but I don't have a racket," I said in my please-won't-you-help-me voice.

Daddy set down his Scientific American, got the car keys out of a brown crock, and drove me in the green Buick down narrow streets shaded by leafy trees to Auburn's hardware/sporting goods/fresh pecans/bait store.

We parked in front. The store owner said he only had one racket, but in his opinion it was just my size, and a bargain at $6.99.

Daddy took seven dollars out of his worn black billfold and didn't mention the price or the racket size. I began my tennis career practicing against the backboard at the college court, where I would arrive with my racket and one brown ball. Frequently, some lone boy would come over and hit with me.

It wasn't until years later that my high school friend Nancy, who belonged to Saugahatchee Country Club, invited me to play. She wore a white shirt, shorts, headband, sneakers, and socks. Interesting, I thought.

But I was puzzled: Nancy had a can that fizzed when she opened it, and if that wasn't enough, three white tennis balls fell out and bounced almost as high as my head.

"Why do you have three white balls?" I asked.

She told me three balls were needed for serving, in case one or the other went into the net, and the balls were white because everything in tennis was supposed to be white. I felt I had graduated up a level.

Being close friends, we laughed at my lack of knowledge, but beneath the humor I cringed. I longed for the day when I would know these things without the gentle guidance of my more sophisticated friends.

Daddy bought me a can of three white balls, and I began to hang around tennis courts wherever I found them, especially in Appleton, Wisconsin, when we visited my grandparents during the summer. Almost like back home, a red-headed boy named Michael who lived in the park next to the court, would mysteriously appear when I was there, and we'd hit together.

I did learn to wear white, but I never could learn to hold more than one ball in my hand at a time. I put balls number two and three in my pockets, one on each side.

If only I'd had a Ouija board, I would have known that this was the beginning of my traveling down a road lined with tennis courts, where small wooden rackets would morph into huge-headed ones, where white outfits would transition into loudly colored ones, and knee-length butchy ensembles would become short and chic.

I still wear white, and I buy a new can of balls when the old ones lose their spring. But to this day, the small-town girl inside of me thinks it sounds just like music to pull off the top of a new can and hear fizzzzz.

LEARNING TO DRIVE

I wanted to get my driver's license in the worst way, but didn't know the gas pedal from the brake. That wasn't going to stop me since driving was such a big deal to me and my Lee County High School classmates. Drive-through restaurants with car hops awaited.

Even better would be squeezing into a car with my friends and going to the drive-in movies. It was only $2.00 back then for a car and its contents, no matter how many people were crammed inside. I don't imagine that included the guy in the trunk, who we'd let out as soon as we parked, but the movie establishment surely knew and didn't seem to be bothered.

"There's an article in *Boy's Life* on stick shifting," Daddy said one Saturday as he turned his crinkly

Atlanta Journal to the science section. "Maybe you'd like to give it a try."

"Can I borrow your *Boy's Life?*" I asked my brother Alan, lifting it out of his hands as he lounged in our living room in the red maple chair. He was reading about what to do if a bear suddenly came toward you.

"Guess so." My four-years-younger brother with his blond curls and blue eyes was so accommodating. I couldn't believe we were related.

The door to the Plymouth creaked and moaned when I opened it. I usually had to put my foot on the running board, lean back, and pull the door open with both hands. Today it opened easily. A good omen, I thought.

I balanced the over-sized magazine on the steering wheel. The cover boasted a man with a taut line catching a flopping trout. I loved to fish with my friend Mac at his family's pond.

The article instructed one to push in the clutch and make an *H* with the stick. Getting into the rhythm, I pushed and pulled the stick until there was no grinding noise, just a smooth gliding sound. I had promised myself I wouldn't eat or sleep until I had conquered the stick.

The magazine said that for reverse one needed to push the shifter down, then right, and pull back. After reading this several times, my impatience reared up. I wouldn't bother with reverse; it was too complicated, and I just wanted to get started. Plus, it was getting late and I feared Daddy might change his mind about going, although he rarely turned down anything I wanted to do.

Daddy drove us to Wire Road, a red-clay two-lane strip on the edge of town. Everyone I knew had learned to drive there.

Daddy and I swapped places, and I jerked the car up and down the hills until finally the shifting was smooth as cream on the milk we bought from a neighbor's farm. "Stay right at all times," Daddy said. "It's my most important advice."

I wasn't listening to him but was busy in my head, planning to show off my future driving license to friends.

"Starting on a hill is so hard," I said, distracted as I tried it. Just then, a car came over the hill. It was driving on the same side of the road I'd drifted into— my left.

"Get to the right. Pull right," Daddy said. He slapped my leg. His glasses bounced off his shirt onto his khaki pants. He stomped his worn work boot into the floor in a stopping reflex.

Fortunately, the farmer was going slowly. He swerved his car in time to avoid an accident.

"Stay right on a hill," Daddy said hoarsely through gritted teeth.

I looked down at the smarting red welt on my leg, dismayed by my carelessness. Tears started rolling down my cheeks. "I'm sorry," I sniffled. I knew Daddy's leg slap was a reflex because he had never done anything like that before, and never would again.

"Park under that oak," Daddy said. He was visibly shaken by our near collision, as was I. We sat in silence. Daddy gasped deep breaths. He snatched out a bandanna and cleaned his glasses, although they didn't seem dirty. He glared up at the oak, seeming to estimate how old it was.

Finally he said calmly, "Toots, why don't you drive home?" And I did. I would never ever forget to stay right. And Daddy never raised his voice to me again.

That summer, instead of going to the movies or playing tennis, I practiced with Daddy almost every Sunday afternoon. I got my license the week I turned sixteen. This was huge. It would mean freedom, I thought.

In actuality, I still had to get permission to use the car. I had to have an awfully good reason for using it. And I had to be home at the agreed upon hour, 10:30 p.m.

On the other hand, there was nothing like driving through town in the sunlight in our Plymouth, waving to friends through the open window, and playing the AM radio just a little too loud.

WAS THE FURNITURE ON TRIAL?

Janet's boyfriend, Sergeant Hank Kistler, was stationed in El Paso, Texas, where she had a baton-twirling scholarship at Texas Western. He had a short leave and was going to spend it with us in Auburn. That meant we had thirty-six hours in which to size each other up. I don't know if anyone else in the family felt pressure, but I did, for Janet's sake.

Hank would be reporting back to his mother, the strong-willed Gretta. She ran Hank's family just as Moms ran ours. We knew that Gretta wouldn't hesitate to put the kibosh on Janet and Hank's relationship if she didn't like what Hank told her. On our side, Moms could do the same to Hank with just a shake of her head.

When Hank opened the front door at 529 E. Samford Avenue, he'd be greeted by a living room sofa, its faded cover and cushions so lumpy that when I sat on it, I wondered if I were sitting on rocks at the seashore and not at home at all. To make matters worse, there was no coffee table or side table on which to set a drink or plate. I usually put my Coke on the rug, hoping no one would kick it over.

On the Thursday before Hank's visit, Moms grabbed her tapestry pocketbook and headed for Grant's Furniture Store on College Street. She pulled open the glass door with the long handle and told Mr. Grant she'd like to try out a sofa, a cocktail table, and an end table. Knowing Moms, she probably started in the sale section first and then sat on every sofa in the store.

Knowing Mr. Grant, he likely had a helper quietly follow behind her to fluff up each set of cushions as she moved down the row.

Then Moms must have given Mr. Grant her I'm-not-completely-sure look. She would have explained to him that the pieces might not be the right size, or might not fit her décor, then probably asked if she could try the furniture over the weekend. Mr. Grant agreed to have the furniture delivered that very afternoon, and he did.

I imagine Moms thought that if she could return the trial furniture to Grants early Monday morning, there would be no charge. She never told the family or the store that those were her intentions, so I couldn't be positive that was what she was thinking.

Friday morning, at ten o'clock, on his normal schedule, Daddy parked his white Ford pickup truck in front of the coffee shop, The Grille. Some folks called it the Greek's, in honor of the man who ran it. As soon as he sat down, Daddy saw a car parked at the bakery nearby. It had Texas plates and an El Paso border rim. Who else could it be but Hank arriving a day early?

Daddy, being a quick thinker, said to the Greek, "I need to use your phone, it's an emergency."

Phones were closely watched over in those days, and of course there were no cell phones.

"Help yourself, Al," said the Greek.

After Daddy had sounded the alarm, Janet went into action. She washed and curled her hair, vacuumed, set the table with Mom's best flowered china, and set out our crystal goblets etched with cotton silhouettes. She had just arranged the flower-embossed silverware when Hank rang the doorbell.

"Surprise!" he said, stepping into the living room. "I couldn't wait to see you, Janet, so I drove straight through."

She beamed. Of course, we all pretended to be surprised at his surprising us.

At lunch, we sat in our usual places: the guest with his back to the front window, Moms and Daddy on the right, Janet and Alan on the left, and I, who requested seeing the outdoors since I loved it so, facing the window. Moms served the company special that never varied—fried chicken, homemade biscuits, green beans with ham hock, and sweet tea. Everyone at the table agreed Moms' meal would get five stars if she were a restaurant.

"Mrs. Smith, may I call you Esther?" Hank asked. Moms blushed. "This is the most wonderful meal I've had since I can't remember when. Your biscuits are as light as a cloud." His cheeks dimpled as he smiled at Moms.

Maybe Hank would be a good choice after all, she was probably thinking. Janet was oblivious to the situation, or maybe she was a good actress. What a relief, both sides have apparently passed the test. We could all relax since things were going so well.

But just as we finished the main course, I saw a white furniture truck with the letters G-R-A-N-T-S slowly going down the hill past our house. Thank God, it's not coming here, I thought. But then the truck stopped. To my horror, it backed up to our driveway, jamming traffic in both directions, and then pulled in next to the stone path leading to our front door.

When Hank wasn't looking, I motioned frantically to Moms. She didn't pay any attention to me. I kept watching Hank and gesturing to Moms whenever he glanced away. Each time my waves were a little more frantic. Annoyed at my distraction, Moms finally looked out the window, paled, and became the picture of how a sea captain must look when she spots an iceberg dead ahead.

Acting calmly, Moms said, "Excuse me," and

strolled in a slow and lazy way into the living room. She pushed open the screen door and dashed out just in time to stop the driver and helper from ringing the doorbell. I followed her out, being curious, and saw her nudge the two men toward the truck so they would be out of earshot of Hank and our family. It was summer and the windows were open to catch the breeze coming down Samford Avenue.

Moms whispered to the furniture store movers to tell Mr. Grant that we had decided to keep the furniture, all of it. "I will buy it and bring him a check this afternoon, or Monday morning at the latest. So you back out of here right now, ya hear?"

The truck pulled slowly out into the traffic again and headed up the hill toward town.

"Who was that?" Janet asked.

"Oh, just some people who needed directions for a furniture pickup. I told them where to go. Would anyone like whipped cream or melted cheese on their apple pie?"

The lunch, which had almost been derailed, continued on to become a rousing success.

A few days later, Gretta and Moms expressed their opinions that Janet and Hank were perfect for each other, and the couple became engaged.

To me, Mom's pronouncement she was buying the sofa and tables was great news. I couldn't wait to invite my friends Nancy, Jane, Joan, Jackie, Jean, Bobby, and Ralph to come over and practice jitterbugging on our living room floor. We'd roll up the rugs, and I could show off our new living room furniture, which blended perfectly with our wood-paneled walls. None of my friends had raggedy furniture and ours had embarrassed me for years, but my friends never said anything, knowing it might make me feel bad. Looking around the room, I felt lighter, like after the spring rains fall, leaving everything fresh and clean. Hank and Janet were getting married. I had my furniture. All was right with the world.

Janet Diane Smith and Henry Evans Kistler, Jr. were married in the Methodist Church in Auburn, Alabama on August 25, 1956. Toots was the maid of honor.

SMELL OF RED CLAY AFTER RAIN

At Lee County High School in Auburn, Alabama, in the 1950s, there was never any mention of black writers or poets. Not that we would have noticed. That's just the way it was. Then one day, our English teacher Miss Rhodes ("Ms." hadn't been invented yet) asked our class, "Who is your favorite poet and why?"

None of us teenagers said anything. To look eager would have been bad enough, but to admit having a favorite poet—impossible. The teasing would have been relentless. But I adored Miss Rhodes and wanted to help her out, so I finally said, "Langston Hughes."

"Why's that?"

"He writes about Alabama and his words sound like music."

The nose tackle football player snickered.

Miss Rhodes gave him a withering look, and he

slumped down, studying the faux wood of his desk with the lift-up top. She would call on him next and ask him a tough question. Anyone with a brain knew that.

"Emilie, can you recite part of a poem?"

> *I'm gonna write me some music about*
> *Daybreak in Alabama ...*
> *I'm gonna put some tall tall trees in it*
> *And the scent of pine needles*
> *And the smell of red clay after rain.*

Braaang, rang the bell to change classes. Nuts, Mr. Nose tackle had escaped.

Miss Rhodes asked me quietly as I was leaving, "Did you know Langston Hughes is a Negro?"

"No, ma'am."

"I hope that doesn't matter to you."

I did think about his being a Negro as I gathered my books, and wondered how I didn't know. There wasn't a picture on the book of poems she had given me, so maybe the librarian didn't know herself. But I think she had decided not to mention his race. I remember when she handed me the book, she had hesitated. I had asked her was there something else.

"No, dear," she had said, "I hope you like his poems," and she turned back to her work.

Thinking back on those days, it was an ongoing decision for a high school student to know when to be straightforward and when it was better to be silent. And, no, Langston being a Negro didn't matter.

As I got older, the thought of what obstacles Mr. Hughes had overcome inspired me to try harder to be who I wanted to be. When I was working as a program director for a cable TV company in New York, I arranged an on-air retrospective with Langston Hughes's family on his one-hundredth birthday anniversary, February 1, 2002. They were dressed in dashikis, spoke of his life and his writings, and I recited my favorite poem, Red Clay after Rain. I felt I had come full circle.

Langston Hughes, Poet and Playwright

UNBIDDEN MEMORIES

I never found out what really happened behind the Piggly Wiggly that Saturday night in Griffin. But as the memory slowly faded, I never expected it would return unbidden.

I was thirteen and had walked a mile to the Tiger movie theater in Auburn with my friend Gary (yes, the basketball P-I-G). We had bought our tickets outside at the glass window and had just sat down as the newsreel came on. The MGM lion roared onto the screen.

An unusually dark and grainy picture came into view. At first it was hard to make out what was going on. Then the picture became sharper. It was night at the edge of woods. A large oak tree loomed over a crowd of milling men. Each man's head was covered with a white hood with eye holes cut out, and white sheets hung like a judge's robe over each body. Only a few carried sticks, but they all wore the same expression—anger.

The picture panned to a rope hanging from a tree limb. Something limp twisted and turned in the wind, twirling back and forth. I felt sick to my stomach. The screen went blank. Perhaps it was the decision of the projectionist who sat above us in a room with a small brightly lit window.

It was always quiet in the theater since no one was allowed to speak. However, this night we heard a wounded sound from above. Until that moment, I'd never thought about there being a separate black section. There must have been a hidden balcony entrance that led in from the alley. I could hear footsteps of people leaving, and couldn't imagine how sick they must feel.

Gary let go of my hand. I asked if he thought we should go home. We decided to stay since we'd already bought tickets with our hard-earned allowances, and we both doubted that our parents would let us come again soon. We sat without whispering, our Tootsie Rolls untouched.

I didn't tell my parents anything about what happened, but this being a small town, I'm sure they knew the whole story before I got back to the house. The theater never showed the clip again.

I had nightmares of that newsreel for a long time. Then it faded away, and once again I hoped those memories would stay gone forever.

TRAIN HEADED FOR SUNSHINE

Daddy and Moms drove me to the Opelika train station with my footlocker filled with clothes for a year at college—I had a complete baton-twirling scholarship. We waited for the Sunset Limited, an express train that stopped only in major cities along the Eastern seaboard railway. Its last stop would be the University of Miami.

Opelika was too small to be a scheduled stop, unless there was a dire emergency. But every night you could hear long-distance streamliners and freight trains blowing their lonesome whistles as they rushed past, sounding like a pack of coyotes howling in the distance.

Despite the prohibition against streamliners stopping, the local train station manager, Mike, had agreed to take his red lantern and flag down the

Limited as it went through.

"Stand on the platform," he said to me. "As it slows to a quick stop, jump on."

Mother gave me $20 to spend on incidentals the first month, since room and board was included in my scholarship. I suspected that $20 for thirty days of incidentals such as books, shampoo, toothpaste, and newspapers was sorely inadequate.

After I settled into campus, I'd start to know the full extent of our underestimation, but that fact was still twelve hours, half the length of Alabama, and the entire length of Florida away.

Around 11:30 p.m.—the train being an hour and a half behind schedule—Mike with his striped trainman's cap came rushing out of the small station, rhythmically swinging his lantern in a half-circle arc, back and forth, back and forth. He was practically leaning over the track.

A lonesome woo, woo followed by three sharp blasts meant the engineer had seen the signal and would stop. If he couldn't see the red lantern, he certainly could have seen my white polyester coat that Moms and I had bought. We imagined it to be the perfect Florida outerwear.

"You can just put it in the washing machine whenever it gets dirty," she explained before I left. "A few quarters and you're good to go!"

I thought I looked like a movie star. I had never seen another coat like it—and I never have since, come to think of it.

The iron train wheels seemed to squeal their distress at having metal brake shoes slow down their wind-splitting race to the glorious sun and palms of Miami Beach. Mike was ready to load my footlocker and I was poised like a runner at the starting blocks, ready to leap aboard. At that moment, the clasps on my overnighter suitcase from the "everything" hardware store came loose. Underwear, pjs, and lipstick spilled on the platform.

"All aboard!" yelled the conductor in a commanding voice. "Leave that stuff and get on the train!"

Scooping up what I could, I ran up the three pebbled metal stairs. "I'll send the rest," Moms promised. I turned around to wave.

"Go on in," hissed Mike from the platform. "This is an unscheduled stop!"

At that moment, I realized my father had talked to Mike on an earlier day, when Daddy said he was going to check the schedules. In a respectful and cordial southern manner, he would have convinced Mike to flag the train, even though flagging was only for dire straits. Money had certainly changed hands. Now it was supremely important to Mike that this stop not delay the train further.

Once aboard, I took a seat by a window and put my much lighter suitcase up on the fancy grillwork rack. I saw another passenger pull down a chrome footrest attached to the seat in front of him, and I did the same. Comfy! The cushion and reclining back were upholstered in an itchy wool fabric. I covered them with my soft polyester coat—it was coming in handy already.

The dining car décor was entirely black, white, and silver. It had white tablecloths and white cloth napkins; the servers had very dark skins, white jackets, and black pants. And there, gleaming on the table, were a heavy silver sugar bowl, creamer, and shakers—heavy to keep them from sliding off. I had a chicken sandwich and a cold, cold glass of milk. A free and scary feeling washed over me. No one needed to tell me to chew my food slowly; I wanted this moment to last forever.

It was a hypnotic ride, looking out the window in the dining car, wheels clanking over the joints in the track, and brakes screeching as we stopped at the few city stations. Bells clanged and lights flashed at rural crossing barricades where a lone car or sometimes two waited. Back at my seat, I dreamed of college boys, football games, and sunshine.

Very early in the morning, we passed orange groves and farms and sometimes barefoot children waving at the engineer and strangers, we who were going by on a train to the city of Miami, a place they had probably only dreamed about. "So have I until now," I wanted to call out.

We arrived in an almost deserted Miami city center

around 8:00 a.m. on a dark, rainy Sunday. A black man in the train station baggage department took my footlocker and locked it in a wire cage, since it would be too heavy to carry with me as I made my way to the Coral Gables campus.

I took my plaid suitcase, which now had a piece of rope the conductor had put around it, wore my white coat against the rain although it was too warm, and went to the bus stop in front that was marked "Coral Gables Route." No buses came in either direction so I hitched a ride, but that is a story for another day.

My new roommate Althea drove me to the train station the next day to get my footlocker. I kept dropping nickels, dimes, and quarters into the porter's outstretched hand, but he didn't make a move to get my bag. I must have hit the magic number, because finally he bent down and lifted the heavy footlocker into the trunk of her car.

How was I to know that each coin was a weight shifting the scale of my future, taking me farther and farther from a home to which I'd only return for visits, like someone passing through on a train bound for distant lands?

Emilie Smith, University of Miami Hurricanette, 1954–56, before transferring to Duke University.

THERE ARE NO ORANGES IN THE ORANGE BOWL

The first time I marched in the Orange Bowl, I had to make a snap decision. I pranced out of the shadowy tunnel onto the football field with spotlights blazing from above. Blinking my eyes, I saw 80,000 people waving pompoms and jumping up and down, chomping on hot dogs and guzzling beer. Coming from a town in Alabama where the entire population, including pets, numbered 8,000, the unexpected cacophony froze me midstep.

Glancing back, I realized there were a hundred band members stomping toward me, majorettes in front. I was about to get trampled by a big guy carrying an even bigger tuba, who was directly behind. As he was about to smash into me, I stifled my fears and strutted ahead. It wasn't a hard choice, as decisions go.

By the next game, the hubbub seemed normal. By the end of the season, it was thrilling. Little by little, bright lights encouraged me to move out of my southern shadow, to participate or to perform, and eventually I learned that if you lead, others will follow.

JANUARY 7, 1955   THE MIAMI HURRICANE

El Salvador Citizens Go Wild Over Band,

PAGE FIVE

Hurricanettes

Emily Smith and Althea Jones examine barriers for parade.

Emilie Smith, left, and the University of Miami band traveled to San Salvador on a good will mission for the U.S. State Department. The barbed wire is for protection, but locals cheered the band at the stadium.

WHO WAS THE MAN IN THE LIMO?

My first real job—one with a salary—was teaching second grade at Holloway Street School in a disadvantaged neighborhood in Durham, North Carolina. To get me there, my car, a second-hander, had made its way from Alabama without breaking down.

Mornings, I parked close to the building to leave space for the children to play. Neighborhood kids in mismatched hand-me-downs or starched dresses and shirts played on what remained of the blacktop.

There was a comforting sameness to the days as I became part of the school community, until one morning a police car loomed in my rearview mirror and followed me into the parking lot. To make things worse, the policeman blasted his siren. It was as if I was back leading the high school band, only this time I was followed by a burly cop with a sunburned neck to match his red hair. Sauntering over to the car he said, "Miss, don't you know your Alabama license tag is expired?"

The truth and only answer that seemed appropriate was, "No, sir!"

"I'm writing you a ticket for a court appearance in two weeks."

And he did. I could only guess what the children would say to their parents that night.

Just then, the scratched and dented aluminum back door of the school swung open, smacking the side of the building. Mary Hamilton, the feisty principal, preceded by her dowager bosom, strode into the parking lot, her face crimson with fury. I felt terrified for the policeman. He looked as if he felt the same way. "Timothy Kelly, how could you?" She couldn't believe he would ticket one of her teachers, especially in front of these impressionable kids. He slunk back to his patrol car and pulled carefully out onto Holloway Street.

None of this did me any good because the pale yellow ticket with black ink was still in my hand.

There was nothing left to do but go to the courthouse on the appointed day. I parked in front of Belk's department store, directly across from the red brick courthouse. I was wearing a respectable navy suit with a white satin blouse, navy open-toed heels, and stockings that had a seam up the back. I straightened the lines of my stockings, pulled open the heavily carved door of the courthouse, and climbed the marble steps to the second floor. The stairs were worn down with a gully in the middle, probably caused by hundreds of the heavy-hearted in scruffy work boots or run-down ballet slippers.

Opening the court office door with its frosted glass window, I showed my ticket to the busy but friendly woman at the desk. "Excuse me, what should I do next and how much will this ticket be?"

"Go into the courtroom and wait for your name to be called. If you're lucky it will be closer to $25 than God knows how much." She turned back to the pile of papers on her desk. Twenty-five dollars was my budget for an entire week's essentials.

The fiftyish judge with a furrowed brow and salt and pepper hair appeared stern but businesslike. He was kind to some and abrupt with others. The only pattern I could see was that extremely respectful petitioners seemed to fare better than belligerents, and a short, organized story was the key.

As I collected my thoughts about what to say, a dark-haired man approached. He wore a suit that looked sleek and shiny; it had vents on the jacket's sides rather than the usual flap in back. His black shoes had just been polished, probably by the shoeshine boy who sat with his brushes, shoe black, and rags on a box in the lobby.

"May I speak with you in the hallway?" he said to

me.

"Yes," I said, startled but curious, and followed him out.

"My boss would like to take care of your ticket."

"I beg your pardon?"

"My boss"—I looked around but he was nowhere in sight—"can guarantee that your ticket will be misplaced in a higher court, and you'll never see it again." He told me to go back and sit down, and the judge would announce that my ticket was being moved up. "Wouldn't you like the ticket to go away?"

"Yes, I would. I really can't afford to pay it." I had noticed that people in North Carolina seemed eager to help teachers. Perhaps they knew how low our salaries were, or they remembered a teacher who had made a difference in their lives. This was exactly what I needed now, some financial assistance. I made up my mind to accept this unknown help.

I sat down on the straight-back oak chair in the courtroom again. The room had groups of people who looked much more economically challenged than I, sitting in ones and twos, most with lawyers who looked economically unchallenged.

Someone handed the judge a note. It could have been about anything, like asking him if he wanted a tuna salad or a BLT for lunch, or maybe like the mysterious man whom I'd never seen before had promised, it was telling the judge to make my ticket go away.

"Docket 2436, Miss Smith, what do you have to say?"

I told the judge what had happened as briefly as I could.

He said, "So you are a teacher at Holloway Street School?"

"Yes sir."

"I know that neighborhood well," he said, handing the clerk a note. "Case held over to the higher court," the judge proclaimed.

Mystified and relieved, I left the courtroom and retraced my way down the worn steps. There was a long black limousine parked in front of the courthouse. It looked official, like a judge's car. But curiously it had no insignia, no title on the side, and no government plates on the back. It seemed to take up half the block. There was not a speck of dust on it, as if it were protected from something so ordinary. A uniformed chauffeur sat in the driver's seat.

As I stepped off the curb to cross, I saw the man in the shiny suit next to the limo. "Hello, again. That went well," he said.

"Yes, thanks so much. I appreciate your friend's help."

I turned to go. "Wait," he said. "My boss"—who was apparently sitting in the limo's backseat behind tinted windows—"was wondering if you would like to have dinner with him tonight. He has a restaurant he knows you'd enjoy."

Lordy, how could I be so naïve? If I got into the stranger's car, I might never be seen again. I felt helpless, as if I were facing this alone, against someone who had all the power. He could buy off not one, but two judges, while I had the power to teach seven-year-olds to read.

Although terrified, I had learned not to show fear when growing up in a neighborhood of boys. I thrashed out the possibilities in my mind. The jealous boyfriend idea wasn't perfect, but the best thing I could think of.

So I took a deep breath and cleared my throat so my voice wouldn't quaver. "Please thank your boss for his kind invitation. But I must tell you, my boyfriend Mike is crazy with jealousy where I am concerned. I don't know what he might do to the gentleman if he and I had dinner together."

The man in the suit looked at me quizzically, as if what I had said was the most fascinating thing he had ever heard. He motioned for me to wait as he spoke with the man in the limo, who had opened his curbside window.

I felt nervous, my face felt hot, and from experience I knew red hives would be starting to splotch there.

Then he walked over and said, "The boss says it's okay."

"Thank you again," I called back as I rushed inside Belk's. I stopped beside the makeup counter to catch my breath, and then I brushed past all the saleswomen in black dresses. I wove around counters and displays, found the rear door, and rushed out, then looked around the corner toward the street and saw that the limo was gone. I crept to the sidewalk hugging the alley wall, just in case.

Once I got inside my car, I locked the doors and thought about what had happened. How did I know it was over, since he could easily find me again?

It was good to get back to my second graders, whom I taught about eggs hatching into caterpillars, which then spun a chrysalis and by metamorphosis turned into monarch butterflies. I brought each model out of a paper bag with a flourish, still unsure of my own flight, but proud as their sweet young faces looked up in awe.

*Emilie Smith graduates from Duke University with a BA in 1958
and a M.ED in 1961.*

HOW WE MET

Dick insists it was fate that brought us together. For him, the saga began when he bought the car of his dreams—a 1958 Triumph 3 sports car convertible. He could have just as easily gotten a new car that wouldn't have broken down. And how did it happen that out of all the marines at Quantico Marine headquarters, Ray Jenkins, his childhood friend from Winchester was now my best friend?

On that fateful Easter Sunday in 1961, Dick's used car did grind to a stop. Ray offered him a ride back to New York where Dick worked. All Ray asked in return was that Dick help escort three Quantico schoolteachers to Greenwich Village. I was one of those teachers.

If Dick had guessed it would kick-start a lifelong

commitment, he might have rented a car instead of buying one, way back when.

For myself, I was looking for freedom. I had come to sightsee in New York to put a notch in my belt of exotic places I'd visited, and to answer the tug of being in the Easter parade.

On Easter Sunday, I wore a pink A-line wool dress in the Jackie Kennedy style, my hair turned under like hers. But instead of her upside-down pill box hat, my hat was covered with subtle shades of pink chiffon roses.

"Isn't this hat a work of art?" I coached my friends.

"Absolutely," they said.

Strangers asked if they could take our pictures. I'm sure it was the hat.

"Y'all sure can," we purred, flattered that someone would want our picture with so many other notable sights in the city.

Having been a middle child, I loved having people notice me, even if it was for a fleeting photograph. I was pleased my picture would go home to different states and maybe even different countries.

Ray decided we teachers had to experience Café Wha in Greenwich Village, the scene for folk music. He had correctly guessed that Southern schoolteachers—Sheila and Susie from North Carolina and I from Alabama—wouldn't venture into Greenwich Village at night alone. The Village had an *anything goes* reputation.

We five ordered hot chocolates heaped with marshmallows and whipped cream, and listened to a black woman stroking the piano keys, singing kinds of songs I'd never heard before. She seemed so different from the Negro women who picked cotton for my father's USDA experiment in Alabama. I wondered how she had the gumption and talent to get a job doing exactly what she loved. I felt a pang of jealousy since I desperately wanted to live in a happening place and be a happening person, doing something I loved. I craved my own audience, in whatever I ended up doing.

At the café, Dick and I talked only to each other. He was the handsomest boy I'd ever met, and had blue eyes the color of a summer sky. I can't remember what we talked about, but I remember thinking it was fascinating.

Then suddenly, I wasn't sure about him. I had to pay for my own hot chocolate. No proper woman ever paid for anything on dates in the South. It had probably been that way since the days before Scarlett O'Hara.

The next morning, the phone in our hotel room rang shrilly above honking traffic outside our sooty window. The insistent ring startled me as I was curling my eyelashes into an upward sweep, readying them for some thick-as-tar mascara.

"Hello!" I said in a syrupy voice.

"Em, would you like to go to lunch?" Dick asked, sounding hopeful.

I asked him how much money I should bring.

But this time he was asking me out. I wouldn't need any money.

At lunch we laughed about the differences between northerners and southerners. He had a different style from most boys I'd known growing up, treating me as an equal and encouraging me to tell him my ambitions. He suggested I think about living in New York. I was unaccustomed to his style and wondered about his motives.

Monday night, Ray and we teachers went back to Quantico. I couldn't stop thinking about Dick. Each day for two weeks I rushed home after school to see if he had called. Boys took the initiative in those days, so I didn't call him. I only planned on being in Quantico for two more months, hoping then to teach in Paris for a year. I was torn between following this dream and leaving behind someone who hadn't even called.

A teaching offer came in from San Diego. That was a lot closer than France, so I accepted. I had hardly had time to put away the French tapes when Dick called saying he had been on a business trip and I should come to New York City for the summer. Work in New York for July and August, my dream destination? I said yes. But I would honor my teaching contract in the fall and wouldn't tell Dick I was leaving until then. Hadn't every town on his business trip had telephones?

In September I left for California to teach. Dick came out for Thanksgiving. I came back to New York for New Year's. Each trip fueled the flames of fate.

And after I fulfilled my California obligation, I came back to stay.

INTO THE TRAFFIC

I drove my old Ford, the color of a lima bean, back to New York City. I was ready to find a New York kind of job, maybe with a famous interior decorator. First, I'd need to look up numbers for employment agencies and make an appointment.

After parking the lima bean, I walked down the street until I found a phone booth. Inside, there was an empty shelf—I guess to put my pocketbook on—but there was no phone book. So I went into a delicatessen, a sandwich shop kind of like those back home, although you couldn't sit down and eat in this one, and the sandwiches were ten times bigger.

I asked the man behind the counter, "Mind if I borrow y'all's phone book?"

"Look in da booth, unda da shelf," he said, pointing to where I'd just been.

"What did y'all say?"

"You got eyes, lady. Did ya look?"

"I looked, it's not in there. Someone musta stole it." That was a good possibility I thought, this being New York City.

"Lady, I gotta store ful uh customers." But he left the store and went out into the booth and asked me, "What borough, lady?"

"What's a burrow?"

"Doncha know where ya wanna go?"

"Right cheer." I pointed to the ground.

He flipped up the largest book, which was attached underneath. Actually, it was part of the shelf. Manhattan was written on the cover. The other hanging books must be the other boroughs. The deli man gave me an I don't believe it look, and muttering to himself hurried back inside the store.

I was thinking, Wow, I've just met a real New Yorker who talks fast and funny.

He was probably thinking, Jeez, I've just met a real hick.

I took out a dime, put it in the phone slot, and made an appointment for a job interview with an employment agency that placed administrative assistants. Even I knew that was a fancy name for secretaries.

The next day, I climbed the stairs to Kelly Girls Employment Agency at Forty-Third Street and Fifth Avenue. A Miss Thompson greeted me and took me into a room where two typewriters sat on chipped tables, scruffy chairs pushed underneath. "Lemme know when you're ready for the test," she chirped.

In those days electric typewriters were used in corporations. Everyone else had a black Underwood like we did at home. When you typed to the end of a line there was a ding, then you'd push a chrome handle to the right, returning the carriage to a clean line.

I tried pushing down on the keys, which felt like they'd been welded in place. Nothing happened! I raised my fingers as if I were playing a piano and smashed them down. Nothing happened! I rubbed my hand around the top and side for a switch.

What if Miss Thompson came back and I was just sitting here? What would I say? I began to feel red splotches starting on my face. Then the door creaked open and another potential secretary came in—a tall gal with teased hair, three-inch heels, and a mouth full of chewing gum. She looked beautiful to me, like my savior.

"Y'all know how to make this thing work?" I asked in a casual voice.

"There a switch under the middle of the right side," she said, and she chomped on her gum. Smack.

Miss Thompson was impressed with my sixty-five words a minute. I told her my dream was to work with an interior decorator. So she scheduled my first interview with Billy Baldwin, the New York decorator. I'd seen his picture and read about Mr. Baldwin in a glossy magazine in the dentist's office back home. Maybe my dream was about to come true.

CLARENCE

Wearing a blue suit and freshly polished pumps, I set out for my first New York City job interview. I was going to see Billy Baldwin, a famous interior decorator whose assistant I hoped to become. His office was set in a three-story house among endless skyscrapers.

I climbed the outside stairs and stepped inside a stylish vestibule. A dumpling-shaped man with crinkly eyes sat on a round metal stool in the elevator. He said he was Clarence and he was waiting to take me up. But he didn't. He fussed with the metal accordion gate, then with the handle, and then rubbed a spot off the frosted glass door, all the while asking me questions.

"Where are you from? Where did you go to school? Why do you want to work here?"

During a lull—since I hate silence—I asked Clarence, "Is this a good place to work?" He nodded. I asked him if he minded being inside all day with so many exciting things happening right outside the door.

"I don't mind."

Since he made no move to take me up, I said, "Ahem," and wondered out loud if Mr. Baldwin would mind if I were late.

Clarence closed the accordion gate, then the metal door, and we started to the top. He asked me to wait in a lush living room where all the furniture matched. He disappeared into an inner office, while I memorized the layout in my mind so I could decorate my future New York City apartment the same way. It would be on a much smaller scale, of course. A few minutes later someone who looked like Billy's picture came floating out.

"Darling, Clarence tells me I should hire you, and he hasn't been wrong yet."

Clarence was the interviewer? Of course, people would have their guard down in an elevator. Now I wanted to work for Mr. Baldwin even more. Billy shook my hand and said, "I hope you take perfect shorthand. My ideas float in and out like bubbles, then poof, they're gone." He waved his hands in the air and gave a good imitation of bubbles popping. I thought he must be excellent at playing charades.

"I type sixty-five words a minute," I said hopefully. But when he asked me, I told him that my shorthand wouldn't meet his standards. So, I didn't get the job, but Billy thanked me for coming in.

On the way down, sniffling, I thanked Clarence for recommending me. "I know you'll do just fine," he said. I wasn't so sure. I slunk toward Park Avenue. My decision to come to New York now felt dumber than dirt.

At an interview a week later, I got a job with Raymond Lowey/William Snaith, an industrial design firm responsible for the look of the Coke bottle, the Studebaker, and the Avanti gull-wing car. Some days the designers would ask my opinion of which examples I liked better. I lived for those days. And fortunately, I didn't know how much I still had to learn. But what I did know was that I was swimming in the bigger pond of New York City, and that I hadn't given up—a resolve I carry with me to this day.

Two Cops, One Fiancé, Two Parents

Dick and I got engaged at the Yankee Kitchen over a bowl of white bean soup, although we'd considered getting married two years earlier. Back then, I'd just arrived in New York and told Dick that I needed to be free and single for a while. Now my fantasies were turning to thoughts of being a bride, romantically living in a new apartment decorated with a Bloomingdale's sofa and all our wedding silver and china. We'd be playing house together. That would surely top city lights.

We decided to drive to Auburn so he could formally ask my father's permission. Since Moms ran the family, Dick would ask her too, probably even first. There was risk involved. Moms had derailed boyfriends of mine she didn't like. Neighbors, and maybe my parents too, had hoped I'd marry a good ole boy from nearby, not a Yankee boy from a suburb of Boston. What would be worse was that we planned to live in Brooklyn Heights but hadn't told them yet. Everything was going to be just wonderful, I knew.

We decided to drive my car to Alabama, since a long trip sitting in his sports car felt like being folded up in an ironing board.

"Just pick me up at the office," he said one day over lunch as we planned our trip.

Was he kidding? I twisted my fingers nervously and reminded him that I'd learned to drive a stick shift on a two-lane dirt road in Alabama, not on six intersecting lanes in Times Square.

"You can do it!"

That's one of the things I liked about him—he thought I could do anything and always insisted I try. In this case it was a stretch, but being too proud to admit it, I rushed headlong past my self-imposed limits.

I began my drive in the relative calm of the Upper East Side, turned down East River Drive, went across Forty-Second Street, and arrived in Times Square. Masses of taxis and buses seemed to be weaving in and out in a dance only New Yorkers could understand. I certainly didn't.

Dick was not on the corner where he said he'd be. Since I had to keep moving, I circled the block, becoming familiar with building façades. After about twenty minutes, I spotted a pay phone at our designated corner. Being desperate, I pulled my car over, punched on the flashers, left the car unattended in a no-parking zone, put a dime in the slot, and called Dick's office.

"He's in a meeting," I was told.

"Get him out," I said—which for me at that time was unusually assertive.

Almost immediately, a policeman pulled up with his lights flashing, got out of his car, and marched up to the phone.

"Lady, you gotta be kidding me," said Officer Riley, after realizing that the errant car was mine. Tears, which had been on the verge of flowing, now came down in gushes. I told the stern-faced cop that my fiancé was supposed to meet me and wasn't here. I hadn't known what else to do but stop and call him.

"Hello, hello," was coming from the phone receiver.

I couldn't hear what Riley said to Dick over the honking horns and screeching brakes, but moments later Dick appeared with his briefcase and his coat half on. He got in on the passenger side and I drove us to Eighth Avenue where I could park legally. We were on our way at last.

While we were switching drivers, a well-dressed man in a blue suit came over and asked Dick directions. Dick repeated them again and again. The man must be an out-of-towner, I thought. Feeling superior, my recent travails faded behind me like a traffic jam that had just cleared.

Several hours later at our first gas stop, we both got out of the car to stretch and Dick reached into his jacket pocket, his pants pocket, and even his shirt pocket to find his wallet. It wasn't in any of them. The person asking directions had been an effective but maddeningly slow pickpocket. Thank goodness I'd brought my wallet, so this time I could pay. We were soon on our way again.

In the middle of that night, when we passed a Valdosta, Georgia, sign, I mentioned that this town had been a renowned speed trap when I'd last driven through from Alabama. It was a subtle factoid and I hoped a warning, but we were just engaged so I didn't want to make a big deal of it.

"Don't worry, honey." Dick pointed out there wasn't a single light on in the whole town. There wasn't. Then suddenly there was. Red-dark, red-dark lights flashed on top of a police car. A small-boned cop who looked as if he would rather be at home in bed under his Lone Star quilt strode up to my car. He had his flashlight on. He'd probably been catching a few zzzzzs when we whooshed by, and the breeze of a Ford going sixty-five miles an hour in a twenty-five-mile zone woke him.

"Don't say a word," I said to Dick, and asked him not to laugh at how strong my southern accent was about to become. "If y'all do, lawd knows what might happen." I mentioned the cop might put a Yankee with a short fuse in jail.

"But … Okay."

"Mornin', sir," I said to the policeman in as cheerful a tone as I could muster, having been asleep myself. I handed him my license, over Dick at the steering wheel, and continued to talk. I told him Dick was my fiancé who was going to Alabama to meet my parents for the very first time. That's why we were traveling so late. I explained to him that when we were leaving New York, a pickpocket had taken Dick's wallet.

"Y'all know what it's like in New York, dontcha?"

He nodded, and then shook his head at the thought of leaving his hometown and moving up north.

"I been payin' for everythin'," I said.

"Where y'all from?" he asked.

"Auburn. Went to Lee County High."

"I swear. I went to college there," he said.

"War Eagle!"

"Right on," he said.

The policeman looked at my Alabama license for a while. "Not gonna give you a ticket," he said, but he told us to switch drivers and not to let my fiancé drive the rest of the way. "Y'all hear me?"

"Yessir and thank you," Dick and I said in a similar but not exact chorus. Officer Jones did that policeman strut walk back to his car, perhaps to get a little more sleep before the sun rose completely over this town which now looked picturesque. I drove until we crossed the Chattahoochee River, separating Georgia from Alabama, at the Columbus/Phoenix City state line, where Dick took over driving again.

At our weekend in Auburn, Dick happened to wear his favorite blue oxford-cloth shirt with its fraying collar and worn elbows, plus his tried and true white tennis shoes that allowed his big toe to poke through the worn spot. I thought that would be a deal breaker, but to my relief, Moms approved of Dick, though in a private moment she thought it was a shame he was so poor. I told her when I had visited his house near Boston, the ancient furniture and wall decorations had been austere and made me think the same thing. It would take me a few years to realize that only a blue blood would know those were a New England sign of good breeding.

Through the weekend, Moms served him extra servings of fried chicken, biscuits, apple pie, ice cream, and, well everything, to make up for what he was probably missing in New York.

Daddy simply said, "If you chose him, Toots, that's good enough for me."

We set the wedding for June 29.

I still like to do the driving when we go south, and not being able to go over twenty-five miles per hour gives me time to reflect on that Yankee Kitchen moment and the trip to Alabama filled with cops. I've never felt nervous driving in a city again, since nothing has topped circling through Times Square on that Friday afternoon. And if a stranger stands too close while asking me directions, I rush away, calling over my shoulder, "I'm late"—which is often the truth.

FOR BETTER OR FOR WORSE

Dick and my wedding was held in the First Presbyterian Church, a two-story white columned structure that looked like something straight out of *Gone with the Wind.* The church that my folks had helped found was deemed to be too small after we sat in every pew and counted the number who could fit.

Guests flew in from California, New York, and Massachusetts, none of whom were accustomed to Alabama's steamy weather. Inside, they joined the southern contingent, and one hundred and fifty people cooled themselves with round paper fans glued to a stick with a funeral home advertisement on the front. I don't know if it helped to move the hot air back and forth near their faces, but at least it was something to do while they waited.

Women had brought hankies in case they teared up

when I walked down the aisle, and, in the meantime, used them to keep the perspiration from running down their faces. Pancake makeup streaked.

Sitting on my side of the church, the left, and on the groom's side of the church, the right, were people who looked very different from each other, save for the fans. They epitomized the Southern and New Englander backgrounds that Dick and I would need to meld together.

In 1963, many Southern women were partial to light flowery dresses and strappy shoes. Some were slightly heavy. It was hard for anyone not to be, after eating our deep-fried everything. Others were blond, thin, beautiful, and sported flaming red lips, fingernails, and toes. My having been away for nine years, I was struck by how attractive the girls looked, like potential Miss America candidates.

Sleek New Englanders on the right side of the aisle were dressed in dark colors, had exquisite haircuts, no nail polish, and pale lipstick, if any. The word *debonair* comes to mind.

The Southerners greeted each other with bear hugs. Really good friends added a rocking side-to-side motion. Some men threw arms around each other's shoulders.

The New Englanders shook hands from a polite distance, seemingly averse to all that hugging and touching. Others gave air kisses on the cheek or nodded their heads.

Everyone waited impatiently for a 7:30 p.m. start. We had chosen that time because there was no air-conditioning in the church, or much of anywhere else in town. My parents and I had thought it might be cooler then. It wasn't.

Daddy took me to the church almost an hour ahead of time. I was often late, but this time we arrived early so he and I could talk alone before I moved away for good. I had so many questions.

At the church, while people sat up front, I asked Daddy if I could see Dick. Against centuries of wisdom of not letting the bride see the groom on her wedding day, they brought Dick into my waiting room. He looked handsome in his white shirt and jacket, his black bow tie, cummerbund, and trousers. He smiled, but then I saw him tug on his ear. I had never noticed that worry crease before.

"This is the happiest day of my life," I gushed to him. I tend to put a Southern spin on everything.

Dick didn't say a word.

I asked him what he was thinking, expecting an equally romantic reply.

He said he was thinking about the responsibility he was taking on.

That must be a New England reply.

I reminded him that I worked too, and could help with the finances. That didn't sound like the old me who wanted a man to pay for everything.

Just then Berkeley, the best man, popped his head

in. "Let's go, Dick, time for the ceremony." He straightened Dick's tie, twisted the cummerbund into place, and then they headed toward a side door near the altar. I could hear them talking about the Red Sox's chances as they disappeared through the labyrinth of hallways.

"Bring back Daddy," I pleaded with my sister Janet, lovely though frowning in her long turquoise dress that had come all the way from Bonwit Teller in New York City.

"Maybe I'm making a mistake," I moaned when Daddy came back into the room.

Without missing a beat, he told me that since there were so many people waiting in the wilting heat, people who had come so far, we should go ahead with the ceremony and the honeymoon.

"If you still feel the same way when you get back, I'll have the marriage annulled," he said.

"Would you really do that?" I asked, doubt creeping into my voice.

"Have I ever lied to you?"

"No, you never have." I knew he was telling the truth; he always did.

"Let's go," he said, taking my arm with authority and heading for the vestibule.

Janet handed me my cloyingly sweet gardenia bouquet; knotted satin ribbons trailed in its wake. She patted the simple but stylish tulle dress I had bought with my own money at Macy's. Moms had insisted I do that since I refused to wear the ruffled, beaded, and pearled confection that was hand-sewn for my sister and suited her, but seemed to swallow me whole.

Daddy and I paused before starting my journey down the aisle and into a new life. We looked at the altar. It was ablaze with candles in four sloping candelabra which gave off more heat than the weather.

Guests were looking at their watches, some whispering, "Seven forty-five?" They probably were wondering if something could be wrong, but switched to relieved smiles as Lowengrin's wedding march began to echo off the walls of the brick church.

As we approached the wedding party, resplendent in their finery and shining damp faces, no one knew Daddy and my secret. He gave me a knowing wink as he sat down by my mother.

Dick took my arm and gave it a squeeze.

After we cut the cake, I overheard Dr. Greenleaf, Daddy's colleague, say that he had always hoped I would marry a local boy, not a Yankee, and that after the honeymoon I'd return to live in Auburn, not Brooklyn. "But now that I've met Dick and his family, I think it's going to be okay," he said.

And it was all right. Daddy, in his wisdom, had given me the possibility of escape that made it okay to enter fully into my new married life.

On our honeymoon in Bermuda, Dick and I rode motorbikes to dinner on the far side of the island, and when I ran off the road, my knee hitting a wooden fence, Dick was there to take me to the Naval Hospital, where they put in six stitches.

Even watching cricket—where nothing seems to happen—was fascinating to me since Dick was standing by my side giving commentary.

And when we came home to a three-room apartment in Brooklyn Heights, the page had been turned and a new chapter started. There would be many more aisles for us to walk down together.

Emilie Smith and Richard Metcalf Spaulding were married on June 29, 1963, in Auburn, Alabama in the Presbyterian Church. Northerners sat on the right and Southerners on the left.

Dick and Emilie Spaulding on
Honeymoon in Bermuda in 1963.

IF YOU CAN'T HANDLE IT

When I was growing up in Georgia, Moms led me to believe I wouldn't become a success like Janet and Alan would be. Since I had Daddy's unwavering support, these comments didn't stick as tight as they might—but I felt them.

I've worked as hard as possible to do something important in Moms' eyes. In the process, I've found I hate to fail even more than I love to win. That has made it impossible for me to admit I can't do something.

The first time I can remember not wanting to be weak was when I was twelve, and Jack, a fourteen-year-old neighbor with spiked hair, tight jeans, and a T-shirt with rolled sleeves, pinned me to the ground and started tickling. I wouldn't say uncle as he demanded, since that would mean giving in, and to a skuzzy boy at that.

Instead, I hit Jack with my fists and yelled stop. An adult heard the commotion and pulled him away. I was too upset to notice who it was, but the person asked me why I didn't just say uncle. I said because that would mean I had surrendered.

I remember Daddy calling Jack's father and telling him Jack should never do that again. And when the father said, "Just tell her to say uncle," I can still hear Daddy tell the man through gritted teeth that Jack should never darken our doorstep again. He didn't.

When Dick and I got married, I was twenty-six and still didn't want to admit I couldn't do everything all by myself. Well, getting help to take off a stuck bottle top was okay, but that was the limit. Jack asking me to say uncle morphed into Dick saying, "If you can't handle it, I'll come and help."

One day our daughter Susie came home from nursery school with a Band-Aid on her forehead. When I ripped it off, a long red gash glared up. We would have to walk five or six blocks to get her stitched—so she wouldn't look like a toughie from the other side of the tracks when she got older—but she, her older sister Amy, and I had just had baths and had sopping wet hair, and there was a howling wind on the frigid Promenade along the East River where we'd walk. Our car would be of no help, being parked under the Brooklyn Bridge, farther away than the doctor.

I called Dick at his office in Manhattan, twenty

minutes by subway, asking him to come and stay with Amy or to pick up the car and drive us.

"We'll catch our death of colds!" I said—another of my favorite Southern expressions.

"If you can't handle it, I'll come and help," Dick said.

I knew that if I said I couldn't manage the situation, he would come immediately.

Click. I slammed down the phone and muttered under my breath, "I'll handle this, and when we're all in the hospital with pneumonia, he can handle it."

Several years later, Dick and I were skiing at Loon Mountain in New Hampshire. We were riding the ski lift to the top of a run called Dead Man's Gulch. Dick had chosen this particular slope because he said, "It doesn't look so crowded."

We found out why as we set off swinging back and forth on the creaking two-person chairlift. Looking up, there seemed to be three options: jumping off the lift immediately while still near the bottom, which I briefly considered; skiing over alternating rocky and icy patches; or schussing straight down a narrow middle trail.

My skiing style, mostly the snow plow, required wide sweeping turns on soft snow with no bumps. I'd never become a great skier since I had only skied briefly while I was teaching in California. Until we moved to New Hampshire, none of the places I had lived—Georgia, Alabama, Florida, or North

Carolina—were known for snow, only New York.

From the top, Dick skied partway down and stopped, showing me the best route.

"Come back and help me," I yodeled.

"If you can't handle it, I'll ski down and take the lift back up and help," he yodeled back.

I was furious. I didn't respond, but started picking my way down.

At one point, an adorable ski-patrol guy cross-hatched his way up and asked, "Are you all right?"

"Yes," I sniffled, which was a lie. I couldn't say uncle and admit I couldn't handle it.

"Good for you," he said quickly before I changed my mind, and he skied on down out of sight.

When I finally got to the bottom and went into the lodge, my face was red from cold and angst. My fingers were frozen. I headed straight for the heated hand-drier in the ladies room. When my fingers had thawed and I had come out, Dick gave me a big hug, said he was proud, and went to the food counter to get me some chili and cheese with lots of packs of free crackers.

Several strangers came up and said, "We were worried about you." They had seen my orange knit geek cap with the upturned bill three different times when they went up the lift, still on the same slope. "Bravo," said another. It's true that I felt secretly justified and proud, but that didn't help me learn to ask for help.

Some years later, on our trek through the Pyrenees of southwestern France into Spain, we came to a spot where there was no guard house and no passport needed to cross the border. We hiked over three glaciers and rocky trails before we stopped for lunch at a mountain hostel, which in France is called a refuge. The waitress signaled that she didn't speak English. As we waited for our soup and Panini sandwiches, Betty, a fellow trekker, showed me the map. The section ahead marked in red said via ferrate—by the iron. This meant we would climb higher via iron ladders or with metal handles bolted into rock.

Since I thought vertical iron ladders were way beyond my ability, I decided to walk the long way, or hitchhike, to our hotel in the next village into Spain. Dick offered to accompany me. The other hikers pretended to understand, although there was an air of "You can hitchhike if you want but we think you're crying uncle," just as Jack and Dick had said out loud earlier. I don't know exactly how it happened, but I had finally gained the self-confidence to know there are times when it's okay to say enough.

Dick and I walked for hours. My legs were burning, so I turned and looked at the driver of a car about to pass. In my experience, a driver in this situation will usually stop and ask if everything is okay, and she did. To our extreme surprise, the waitress from lunch called out, "Would you like a ride into Spain?" She appeared to have learned perfect English in the short time since she had served us. I wondered what language method she had used, perhaps un joli pourboire—a good tip.

Later that afternoon, when our intrepid hiking friends straggled in, they said that perhaps I'd made a good decision. But the next morning when I got on the jitney bus early, before our hike on a different mountain, the driver mentioned to me that the go-ahead guys had been grousing that I had taken a ride. The driver said he told them they were out of line. First, in that section of France, no one ever stops to pick up a hitchhiker. Getting someone to give me a ride was impressive. And admitting I couldn't do something took more strength than pretending otherwise. "*Il ne pas en la tête*—don't take yourselves so seriously," he had told them.

I thought I'd take his advice as well. Not taking myself so seriously allows me to ask for help most of the time. The hardest, of course, is letting my husband think I'm anything but superwoman.

THE ONE I LEFT BEHIND

It was on a Friday that I, a woman in her early thirties, abandoned Kristiana, our three-month-old baby. It wasn't in an auspicious place: the Key Food store. Boxes crammed the tiny aisles, but there was an empty spot up front where you could leave your baby carriage while you shopped. That's where I left her.

Once finished shopping, I headed across the street to the corner of Hicks and Henry, pulling my wire grocery cart filled with the week's groceries, clean laundry, and dry cleaning. Amy, five, held on to the cart while I held the hand of Susie, four. When we got home, I put the key into the large brass lock of our apartment building. Shuffling around three kids, laundry, and groceries at the same time seemed to be getting easier.

It was then that I noticed the baby was missing.

Panicked, I asked Amy," Where'd we leave Kristiana?"

"At the grocery."

"Why didn't you say something?"

"You have Susie and me."

I locked the two girls in our second-floor apartment with boxes of animal crackers for entertainment and raced like a crazy person back across the street, thinking, What if she's not there? God, don't let me down now.

I stopped outside the grocery, breathing deeply. At least there were no police cars at the curb—yet. I rushed inside. The carriage was still there. Who was that shapeless form leaning over it? I moved closer, holding my arms out to block its escape with our precious baby.

When I got closer I could see the form I'd feared was a kindly looking woman who was jiggling the handle. She seemed surprised that I was coming in the door, not from the rear of the store, and she probably wondered why I was running like a fullback. I muttered thanks and hurried back home with Kristiana.

I had always heard the expression, "You don't appreciate what a special thing you have until you almost lose it." Now I knew what that meant. I rocked Kristiana longer than usual that night, put the older girls in their pajamas, and sang them gospel songs until they and I were asleep.

I frequently think it's so hard to get things right as a

parent. But I must be getting better—I never lost a child again.

First rent–controlled apartment, second story right, three rooms for $150/month.

WE CHOSE DIVERSITY

The night after I left Kristiana in the grocery store, Dick told me he wanted to move out of the city. He pointed out I wouldn't have to move the car for alternate side-of-the-street parking—we'd have a driveway. I wouldn't be walking in the rain with three girls, groceries, and dry cleaning—I'd park in front of stores. We wouldn't be paying tuition—the girls would go to public schools.

Having been in New York for eight years, I was appalled by the idea. I thought myself a sophisticated superwoman who went to plays, museums, and window-shopped at Cartier's. I was stylish, knowledgeable, and had a dab of debonair. I worried the suburbs wouldn't support my progress and would end my love affair with the twenty-carat orange diamond I imagined sneaking out of a locked case in

Tiffany's, wearing it around the store, then returning it to its satin cushion.

Were it not for the nagging guilt of having left our baby, not even Moses could have made me agree to go.

We decided to begin our house search in neighboring Westchester County by finding an area that was similar to Brooklyn Heights—a white-collar, closely knit neighborhood filled with well-educated people. We looked along the Harlem train line at a town twenty-five minutes out of Grand Central, a quick commute for Dick. Our plan was to look at houses for sale, and if we found something, I'd ask a local person where we should we eat to get a feel of the town's ambiance. "We're planning to move here," I'd say.

The first person I asked when we landed in Bronxville, a smartly dressed woman walking her labradoodle, said, "Go to The Field Club." The waitress was cordial, the meal delicious, and the people attractive. They were so upscale that they barely moved their lips when they spoke. When I asked Dick if everyone in town was British, he told me it was called a finishing-school accent.

"I might not feel comfortable here," I said.

Then, remembering my experience with separate water fountains, separate schools, and separate neighborhoods, we decided to drop train times as a criterion and seek a diverse community. It took nine months. Dick liked Hastings, I liked the Tarrytowns. Whichever homeowner accepted our bid first would decide where we'd live. The Tarrytowns won.

Before signing a contract, I met with the superintendent of schools, who said all sorts of families lived in the area, from those who commuted to the city to those who were employed at the General Motors plant. Furthermore, the school district embraced the Princeton Plan: all students were bused to elementary school in one neighborhood, to middle school in another, and to high school in a third. They learned to like and accept each other.

Class photos looked like a junior United Nations. Friends had last names that we had to learn to pronounce. All three girls credit their early school experience for their feeling of being at home with diverse people and languages. Scratch the surface and you'll find a family member who speaks French, Russian, Spanish, Chinese, and, of course, Southern.

How fortunate that The Field Club diners had spoken with finishing-school accents. Who knows what opportunities our girls might have missed if we have chosen a mini-commute over a melting pot.

Emilie hosts a program for teachers with
C-Span and Cablevision in Yonkers, New York.

DROP THE KEYS

When we moved to the suburbs from Brooklyn Heights in 1971, we had one car. I drove Dick to the Philipse Manor train station only if he didn't have time to ride his bike. That was easy enough to do.

"Wake up, I'm late," he said early one hot June morning. I jumped out of bed in my summer nightgown. While he drove, I combed the tangles out of my hair. Since none of our neighbors would see anything else of me, I thought that was good enough. At the station, as the car rolled to a stop, Dick jumped out with his briefcase, running to catch the train, which blew its whistle as it rounded the bend.

I immediately threw my leg over the stick shift to climb into the driver's seat without having to set foot outside in my see-through skin-colored nightie. To my horror, I noticed there were no keys in the ignition.

Dick must have taken them through habit.

All I could think about were my poor girls unfed at home who needed breakfast and encouragement to catch the bus on time. That thought alone helped me jump out of the car. Calling to Dick as he ran over the metal bridge to the far track, I yelled, "Drop the keys!"

"What?" he asked as he hurried along, glancing back from the approaching train, whose brakes were now squealing.

Since he hadn't seemed to understand the urgency, I rushed up the overpass steps yelling, "Drop the keys!"

"What?"

"She said drop the keys," shouted a man with a deep voice, now running behind Dick to catch the same train. I hadn't noticed him before. He didn't look at my face and I didn't look at his. Dick dropped the keys on the pedestrian bridge.

I slid back into the car, hoping the girls were getting dressed. Very soon the platform was empty, so I jumped out, scooped up the wayward keys, and made it home in time to hand each of the girls a warm Pop Tart. I hugged them good-bye and sent them to catch the orange Tarrytowns school bus that was approaching our corner.

As I enjoyed my first cup of coffee, lightened to exactly the same beige color every morning, I hoped none of their teachers chose this day to ask the class what healthy things they had had for breakfast.

For the next thirty-five years, I never drove to the

train station unless fully dressed—with my usual makeup of eyeliner, blush, and lipstick. Or at least in a bathrobe. So, of course, Dick never again took the keys.

HOT COAT, COOL COAT...
EARLY BIRD SPECIAL

Our three daughters have only known living in the cold, having been born in Brooklyn. First they rode in a pink hand-me-down baby carriage I borrowed from Janet. Then, as they grew older, they walked side by side on the Brooklyn Heights promenade. In winter, this stretch was a particularly frigid balcony running along the East River. Scraps of paper would swirl and dance in the wind, reminding me of when I was the drum major prancing on the high school football field on Friday nights in Alabama.

Through it all, I wore a thin brown coat with one large button—stylish in the '60s—which frequently blew open when caught by the wind's icy fingers. I craved a fur coat that buttoned all the way down, which would leave my hands free to dab the kids' runny noses.

Dick and I thought a fur was too much of a luxury on his publishing salary. I had stopped teaching to take care of the three girls, who were born in a span of four and a half years.

"Hooray," I shrieked to myself after spotting an ad in the classifieds: Fur coat, $150. Phone 212 555 furs. Nothing more. It read like a ransom note. I called that number as fast as I could turn the rotary dial, since the price was ridiculously low and I could afford that amount out of my grocery budget.

A woman with a tired voice said the coat was truly $150 and she asked me to meet her in the lobby of the Bossert, a marble-floored hotel turned shabby. I could see the building from the kids' bedroom window.

The hotel had fallen into its hardscrabble state when New York City mayor John Lindsay, who lived in a brownstone several blocks down, had decided to use it and similar hotels to house welfare families. It proved to be an economical way to put up the homeless, but it came at a price. Kids hung out on the street and seemed to never attend school. Families sat on stoops under our fire escape windows drinking beer every night, their raucous laughter squeezing through the gaps in our bedroom window frame. At first, the sounds annoyed me when I got up to feed the baby every four hours. Then one night, their singing sounded fun, and I felt a tinge of envy at their freedom. Empty whiskey bottles lay scattered on the gray sidewalk as I passed in the morning, walking Amy to Montessori school.

The Bossert lobby was not a logical place to be buying a fur coat, but I blocked that thought like a nose tackle protecting the quarterback. When I entered the dingy stone vestibule with its tall dirty windows, a worn-looking woman in her forties held up a muskrat coat and said, "I can't afford this anymore. I've come upon hard times." That appeared to be the case.

She wanted cash, but I only had a check from the bank up the street. Hurriedly she took my check, phone number and address, and started for the door.

To make her feel better, I said, "Thanks, I'll take good care of your coat." She strode away shaking her head.

The phone was ringing when I opened the door to our apartment. It was our bank calling to make sure the person with my check was legitimate. They were skeptical, until I abruptly, for me, thanked them for calling and asked them to give her the cash.

When Dick came home that night, he questioned me about exactly where the coat might have come from, though to his credit he stopped when he saw my bubbly happiness begin to fizzle.

Eight years later, in 1971, the fur was getting worn around the cuffs and neckline. You might say it looked bedraggled from making trips to the playground, grocery, and bank, or from being on top of my side of the bed midwinter when Dick decided we should sleep with snow drifting in the open windows.

The coat's wear and tear made no difference to me, but made it feel like an old friend. It was the first thing I packed when we moved to the suburbs of North Tarrytown. We'd saved enough in eight years of living in rent-controlled apartments to make a down payment on our first house. And though I left the city kicking and screaming, I knew in winter I'd be wrapped in my aging fur, able to explore our four-bedroom colonial in its warmth, and begin to learn the winding roads of Sleepy Hollow Manor secure in its comforts.

A month after we moved, the fur and a wooden jewelry box made by my father-in-law were stolen from our new house. Seeing every drawer overturned, mattress covers thrown back, and half-eaten candy littering the rug—the police said this was a sign of drug use—I raced into the bathroom and threw up. We had never had a robbery in Brooklyn.

We considered getting a burglar alarm, but a neighbor suggested we leave the light on in the kitchen, a radio playing loudly to a talk show, and a large toy on the front walk. Her advice worked for the next thirty-six years, until we retired and moved to New Hampshire. The North Tarrytown police called me frequently describing furs they'd recovered, but none was ever mine.

Politically, it wasn't a good time to wear fur, and I gave up the idea of ever having a fur coat again.

It wasn't until twenty years later when Dick took

me out for dinner to the Tarrytown Hilton on my birthday that the subject arose again. He wanted to go to dinner early, probably so we could get the early-bird discount on our meal. I was incensed that my parsimonious husband, with his you-might-call-it-frugal background if you were being kind, or stingy if you weren't, would even consider skimping on my birthday.

The grandfather clock in the lobby of the Hilton had just dinged 5:30 as we arrived. We were seated, and soon a mouth-watering dinner arrived accompanied by white wine in sparkling glasses, a candle-lit dessert, and the end of my tiff. All I could think about was a carefree night without kids.

Walking to the hotel lobby about 7:30, I noticed a beautifully lettered sign announcing a fur sale in the ballroom. It was to end at 8:00. I talked Dick into going in so I could try on some furs for fun. "It's so early," I said. What could he answer?

Dick didn't protest. On a lark, I headed straight to the back of the ballroom where chained platinum-colored coats hung in a glass case. The long numbers on the price tags hanging from the sleeves took my breath away. I looked terrible in them, like a housewife playing dress-up in a movie star's coat. My hair wasn't poufy enough, my fingernails weren't long enough, my polish wasn't red enough, and my heels weren't high enough.

As we headed toward the door, Dick let out a sigh

of relief. He shouldn't have, for as I was almost out the door, I spotted a rack of specials. A brown fur with a silver and brown ruff circling the entire front edge seemed to be calling my name. Slipping the coat on made me feel like a million dollars.

"Kozji krasivj." An older man, who had been meandering around the beautifully wallpapered ballroom, had raced over and spoken.

"Fur is beautiful," his younger friend translated.

"Sovershena," said their colleague. Stitched perfectly.

"Ne doraga." Not expensive.

"Zjena prekrasnoj." She looks lovely.

"Kupite palto." You must buy it.

"Would you believe it's my birthday?" I asked. The young man translated, and the three kissed their fingertips and lifted them toward me. So sweet and convincing they were.

Dick thought they might be shills and expressed that thought aloud, attempting a lighthearted manner. But the young man's face flashed red, and so did mine, and then the man said in almost perfect English, "We come from Russia, for conference. We become entrepreneurs—the American way."

So Dick bought me the coat without further hesitation, perhaps with only a whimper. It was a stunning coat and made me feel warm and elegant when I wore it.

Poor Dick, he later saw the humor in it all. If we

had come at the regular dinner hour, the fur sale would have been closed, and he could have saved much more than he saved by taking me to the early-bird special.

When people ask me where I got my beautiful mink coat with the fox collar, as they invariably do, I mysteriously say, "Dick bought it for me at the early-bird special. Isn't he the sweetest?"

Dick's looks-to-kill come next. Then he and I laugh. The others wonder what the joke is about, but I've learned not to tell. Enough is enough. And at last, I once again have a very warm coat to wear during long winter months.

"Hot" Coat from Brooklyn
with Susan and Amy

"Cool" coat from Tarrytown.

TAKE THIS JOB AND LOVE IT

Kristiana clambered onto the yellow and black school bus headed for kindergarten. She wore a Swedish sweater, Scottish kilt, and Dutch haircut. I waved good-bye much too eagerly to our third and last child. I felt like a football player celebrating a touchdown. I'd been at home with three kids for fifteen years, which added up to 16,425 meals, 825 loads of laundry, and 72 school conferences.

There was an eerie quiet around the bus stop. I noticed mothers and fathers of first or even second children standing under the beech tree tearing up while taking pictures. They looked at me as if I were unfeeling. I tried not to grin. I sympathized since I had felt that way myself—twice—but not now.

With Amy and Susie, I'd followed Dr. Spock's baby book verbatim, but with Kristi I used a simpler scheme of child raising: expressing love, boosting her confidence, and encouraging her to care for others, which was her natural temperament.

Hugging her in the morning, I'd say, "Do you know how much I love you?"

"Yes."

"Do you know you can be anything you want?"

"Yes, you told me that yesterday and the day before."

"Will you be kind to everyone?"

"Sure."

"Here comes your bus. 'Bye, sweetheart."

Watching the bus pull away, I felt like a Sing Sing inmate walking to freedom. I didn't know in which direction to head or how hard it would be to choose to move beyond my committees and find a new career. My euphoria evaporated.

Since Kristi had started lower school two years earlier, I knew I didn't want to go back to teaching kids the same age as she, and I also knew that I wanted to start getting paid for my work.

What-am-I-going-to-do kept coming into my head like a mantra gone astray.

Neighbor Joby, sensing my feeling of being adrift, invited me—more like insisted—that I come that very weekend to a workshop at Skidmore College called Find Your Design. "It's right up your alley," she said.

We drove two hours north before arriving at her alma mater in the early evening. Pulling a book out of her suitcase, she said that participants were supposed to have already read the book.

"I didn't tell you because you might not have come."

Was she kidding? It wouldn't have mattered. I would have done anything to find my way through the thicket. I had told anyone who'd listen, and a lot who probably didn't, that with all three girls in school, I was going to make my big move. This was my surefire way to make myself follow through. I still couldn't bear the thought of being called a quitter.

Lying under a lacy canopied bed in an overheated room in the Alumni House, I started reading. A starry night bodes well for the next day, I've always thought, and the sky outside was ablaze. Years before I had learned Evelyn Wood's speed-reading method: You run your finger down the center of the page, reading each line, without glancing side to side. Do it until you can read straight down without your finger or your eyes moving back and forth.

The reading was going well except for one problem. I wanted to be Barbara Walters, who in front page news had just contracted to make a million dollars. It may be hard to believe, but the amount of money didn't interest me as much as being in the spotlight. I pictured myself on TV, peeling back my guest's personality like the skin of an onion, and exposing their special nature for the world to see. Perhaps Moms would be proud.

My newly discovered direction was contrary to what I'd learned at the brick church atop a hill in Auburn, Alabama, where serving people had been my goal and the reason I'd become a teacher. Greatness to me then would have been becoming superintendent of schools or discovering a cure for a disease, as Jonas Salk had recently done with a vaccine against polio, or something in between.

That night, sleep refused to come. Tossing to the right, twisting covers around to the left, I felt relieved when the sun finally shone through the leaded glass window. At 6:00 a.m., jumping out of bed in search of coffee in the conference room, I found a kindly looking middle-aged man putting out worksheets.

"What are you doing up so early?" he asked.

"Couldn't sleep. You?"

"Me either." He said he was the author and facilitator. Figures he wasn't the cleaning person since he didn't have a bucket and rags and besides, he looked more like a professor. We talked for a while, and I told him about the kind of success I wanted to achieve.

"Believe that you can and you will," he said. Then he asked me to come and see him at the end of the weekend and tell him that's what I was going to do.

Besides reaffirming my desire to become an interviewer, by the end of the workshop I had learned that I liked to be given a goal and to be left alone to reach it. I preferred to use social skills to get others to do what I needed, rather than use mathematical ones. Most importantly, I knew my real goals, not the ones I'd been taught I should reach for.

Before we left, the leader hammered home his overarching theme: success is about doing exactly what you want to do.

On Sunday, as I was collecting my things, the author came hurrying toward me. "Are you still going to be Barbara Walters?"

"Yes!"

What else could I say to him?

If there had been a crystal ball to gaze into, I would have seen that I would begin as a cable TV interviewer and then move into better and better jobs.

For the next twenty-six years, I raced out early and eager to start my day, thanks to Joby and the workshop where I found my design.

Kristiana as a bridesmaid in her cousin Victoria's wedding.

LET'S DO LUNCH

Once back home, I wondered that I'd blithely promised the trainer I'd get a job as an interviewer on TV. I always did what I promised, but this time I needed encouragement, and professional advice might give me the confidence I needed.

So, I signed up for another workshop. This one was a day-long affair at the Waldorf Astoria in New York City and was entitled, How to Get the Job You Know You Want. I couldn't believe the ad was real. The subject was just what I needed and when I needed it.

The deal proved genuine when I got to the hotel early and sat next to Kevin, the leader, in a soon-to-be-filled circle. "Before we begin," he said, "let's talk about what you think you should do to get the job you want. Emilie, start."

That is the danger of being early and appearing

eager. You're usually are asked to go first.

"Well, uh." I told the group I would take the person-in-charge of hiring out to lunch and find out everything I could about the company and the job. Then I'd mention the coincidence that my qualities matched their needs, saying, "Perhaps you should hire me," and I'd smile in an offhanded way.

"Ha, ha, ha, that's so funny," the five other students said, seeming to laugh forever.

I could feel hot spots on my face. I didn't understand their amusement then, and I still don't, since doing lunch is a Southern solution for almost every situation. As we continued around the circle, others had more traditional ideas that no one laughed at, to my dismay.

At the end Kevin said, "Those were all excellent. But I hope you have the courage to go back and do what Emilie suggested. The company might just offer you the job."

The others looked at me the way we sixth graders used to look at the teacher's pet who always had her hand up.

The next morning, before I lost my nerve and knowing that I wanted to work in the media, I headed straight for The Journal News. It was a job possibility and a test run, since my goal was to be on television. I wouldn't be going in cold, since I'd recently received a lot of exposure as the only female elected official in the Village of North Tarrytown.

The newspaper offered me a job covering political meetings, mostly at night, at a salary of $14,000 a year.

"Thank you so much. May I think about it?"

My next stop was the radio station, located in a round yellow building that looked like a wheel of cheese. Though a great friend of mine, the owner was patriarchal and unbending in his opinions. A voice in my head said, You are not a good fit, get back in the car. So I did and drove to the cable TV station. It may be hard to believe, but my voices usually give me solid advice.

I got to Tarrytown at just after 11:00 a.m. Was it possible Garrett, the cable TV program director, would want to go out to lunch that day? I had $6 in my billfold and many of the local cafés accepted cash only. I got back in the car, drove to the bank, and asked the teller for $100.

"Hi, Garrett," I said, walking into the studio. McLean Cable took up a squatty stucco building, a former bakery, at the bottom of a parking lot off Broadway. "Do you think you might let me take you out to lunch sometime to get your advice about working in cable TV?" I asked.

Garrett, thin with sandy brown hair, was my height. He stood up and put on his suede jacket, the one with elbow patches. "How about right now?" he said.

There is a God, I thought, feeling the $100 in my pocket.

During lunch, I asked him questions about himself,

his goals for covering the community, and the good and bad parts of the job. Mostly, I listened. And how could we not become friends while sharing a meal together?

Roger, the owner of the cable company, called me early the next week and asked me to work without salary for two months, so he could evaluate the fit. I took a deep breath, pretending to consider his offer without waiting too long, and then agreed to his nonsalaried proposal.

I don't know when I learned that getting my foot in the door was key. Working hard afterward was easy. I'd learned that from my German grandparents.

A few months later, Garrett left and Roger asked me to open a new community channel. I would be interviewing guests on the air. I thought I must be dreaming—becoming my own version of Barbara Walters. Don't anyone pinch me and wake me.

YOU'RE ON THE AIR

Glamour is not as easy as it looks. Take TV interviews. I thought they would be like gossiping with friends—and in some ways they were. I'd known that game since kindergarten. But the rules for my new job were Greek to me.

For my first interview, Mayor Pillar of Tarrytown and I sat in a studio in comfy chairs under lights hot enough to sunburn a snake. We leaned in toward each other. I wearing my new navy dress and shoes, and he was wearing his worn navy suit and tie.

"Five, four, three," the floor manager said, and then there was silence.

"What happened to two and one?" I asked in a strong voice, trying to sound confident in the face of complete bafflement.

Dan, the director, told me that the last two numbers are unspoken so the sound wouldn't ooze onto the tape. "Rewind. Take two," he said.

When his finger came swinging down this time, I said, much too enthusiastically, "Welcome, Mayor." He almost jumped out of his seat.

Once, during a different interview, I said I didn't know if we'd have a rate increase, and I rubbed my hand on the side of my nose. The director whispered in my earpiece that I was signaling a lie. I corrected myself and said I didn't know *when* we would have a rate increase, but there would be one in the future. Who knew body language was as important as the words.

No matter how experienced I became, the crew and I lived with uncertainty. Our studio had no bleeper delay. What anyone said from home went on the air unvarnished. One Thursday night a distressing call was directed at a different local mayor, a woman. The caller falsely told the screener in the control room that he wanted to talk about zoning. But what he actually said was, "Why is the mayor so fat?"

I opened my mouth and moved my lips, but nothing came out.

We filled the half hour, went off the air, and I apologized to the mayor.

"Don't worry, it's not your fault," she said. "That was my ex-husband."

As being on TV became more routine, the crew and

I became more creative. When the General Motors manufacturing plant closed and thousands were out of work, we produced and aired a free commercial for former workers. The program was featured in the New York Times, they became local TV stars, and many got new jobs as a result.

And every time I heard that opening count down—five, four, three, plus two seconds of silence—I'd remember my first day in the studio, and a smile the size of Tennessee would spread across my face.

"What's so funny?" the crew would ask in my earpiece. I never told, since I didn't want them to know that if you scratched my surface, a country girl still lurked underneath.

Emilie and officials on Election night, 1982, in
McLean Cable TV studio in Tarrytown, New York.

Hair Today, Gone Tomorrow

The hardest part of being on TV, for me, was looking the part—wearing a business-like dress or suit, having a sleek hairdo, manicured nails, and in case the camera pulled out to a wide shot, polished shoes.

One particular Thursday, leaving the office around 3:00 p.m., I looked in the rearview mirror of my Karmen Ghia convertible, inherited from my father-in-law. My hair looked like Texas tumbleweed.

I saw a second floor sign just up the street. It had silver lettering and read "Serendipity Hair Salon." I wheeled into a parking spot and clomped up a set of creaking stairs, opening a door to a fancy but almost empty salon.

The interior was black, white, and silver with a single red rose on the reception desk. It looked like the Elizabeth Arden salon in New York City.

I put on my I-need-a favor voice and said to the hairdresser, "I'm going to be on TV tonight and my hair is a fright. Would you please cut it?"

"Would you like an appointment?"

"Could you possibly cut it right now? I would be most grateful."

"Emilie," said Pierre, whose name was on the door, "I'm closed on Wednesdays."

He was probably thinking, I must remember to lock the door on my day off and how will I get her down the stairs and out of here?

But how had he known my name? I asked.

"Whenever I see you on Cable Talk, I always say to my partner, oh dear, her hair is so wrong."

He studied me, then said, "If you let me cut your hair any way I want, I will stop paying bills right now and do it."

I was so flattered that he watched my show.

Pierre cut my long hair an entirely new, slightly shorter style.

"No, that isn't quite right," he said, frustrated.

The cuts kept getting shorter and shorter.

"Fini!" he finally exclaimed.

I was afraid to look in the mirror. My face always telegraphed my true feelings. So I looked down, which was worse. The floor was almost entirely covered with all different lengths of my frizzy hair. Frizzy because stick-straight hair like mine was out of style, so I got a perm every four months.

I was relieved that Pierre charged me list price and not for three haircuts and two hours of his time. Thanking him profusely, I raced home and looked in the mirror. The very straight, very layered, and very short cut looked … chic, I said to myself.

Quickly changing into my on-air outfit—a blue silk dress—I raced back to the studio where the crew said, a little vexed, "Where have you been?"

Then, "Wow."

Since we thought Pierre might be watching the show (and his haircut), the crew typed in a credit for the salon. It became a permanent fixture in the rolling credits at the end of the show.

While doing interviews, I had more confidence knowing my hair was up-to-date.

Best of all, I never had another perm. I didn't miss the stinky curling solution that always ran down my neck and took the color out of whatever I was wearing.

And now I had a personal understanding of the word serendipity after finding a salon by that name. Probably to everyone's fatigue, I used the word relentlessly for about a month or two. I stopped by the time my hair had grown long enough for me to rush back for another Pierre cut.

Hair today, circa 1984

Gone tomorrow

SING SING I

When an acquiring company decides to take over a smaller company, no matter what their good intentions are, choosing which employees to keep is like picking a sports team. Which do you play and which do you leave behind on the bench? In the first of two buyouts I was involved in, American Cablesystems was buying McLean Cable, my original cable company, for a rumored $17,000,000.

I thought my chance to stand out from the crowd was to contribute a special program that would make a solid mark on the community. I found that chance when I stumbled upon the new company's public relations program—Reading Is All American, a literacy campaign. I'd taught second graders in four states how to read, and nothing in teaching matched being present when someone exclaimed, "Lookit me,

I'm reading."

Our regional headquarters was in Ossining, New York, and nowhere was the inability to read more widespread than among the inmates of its infamous prison, Sing Sing. I cold-called the warden, made an appointment, and got his support to hold a literacy run inside the Yard. We would work with literacy volunteers to raise money for books and a reading program there. It was a forward-looking idea for a prison. I'd never heard of a run for literacy inside a prison.

The warden told me that 67 percent of the inmates couldn't read. He thought that might contribute to why the men wound up in Sing Sing in the first place and was sure that it made it harder for them not to return.

We sent out letters to donors, met with prison staff, and contacted TV networks and newspaper outlets. Just as I was thinking my tenure at the TV station was assured, the wheels came off my literacy bandwagon. Everyone had responded excitedly—except key potential donors.

With a steely clang in their voices that matched prison doors closing, donors told me they didn't want to put money on murderers. Many were upset that their taxes already paid for prisoner incarceration. They were not in the mood to see the logic of teaching prisoners to read.

Whatever would I do now? Send out a press release saying, "Oops"? Then type and send around my job résumé? I felt like a condemned woman anxious to escape my fate.

I made a cold phone call to George, the new company's public relations person in Massachusetts. He knew I was a jogger and asked, "Why don't you run?"

Me, run in my shorts and T-shirt in Sing Sing prison with murderers?

It did sound better than confessing that I'd failed. I pictured Moms saying, "I told you so," to Daddy.

George suggested I should find other runners as well, who could convince friends to pledge money on them. I would do the same.

Friends and cable TV employees pledged generously toward my running, joking that it would be "great to have you in prison, maybe they'll keep you there." Well, I think they were joking. My husband lent his wholehearted support, and I flectingly wondered if he also had an ulterior motive, perhaps to stop my complaining about how he didn't load the dishwasher right?

The dollars started coming in. Even New York State Supreme Court Judge John Carey who'd read about the run joined us.

ABC, CBS, NBC, and other national media called to say they would be sending TV crews. I was elated. Surely, I was doing a notable thing and my job was safe.

We were to run on a Saturday. On Friday, as I was

setting out my running shorts, wick-away T-shirt, and comfy sneakers, a news announcer broke in on my bluegrass radio program with the announcement that a 747 jetliner had been hijacked. Passengers had become hostages and the plane had been diverted from New York City to Cuba. All networks took to the skies to cover the event.

I was fearful for the passengers who had been kidnapped and flown to a foreign country, and sorry for their families. And I felt sorry for myself, having my good-intentioned efforts hijacked as well. My fear of failure now trumped my fear of being in prison with murderers.

When I called them, United Press International (UPI), the Associated Press (AP), and the Ossining Citizen Register said they would still send reporters and photographers. By morning, the run was back on track.

On the actual day, I was anxious as I drove myself the five miles from my house to the harsh-looking building on a hill overlooking the Hudson River. The prison doors with thick metal bars sliding shut behind me sounded final. A burly guard took my briefcase, and our footsteps echoed as he led me toward the exercise yard. I felt a heaviness on my chest and wondered if it was the weight of generations of prisoners whose spirits had never left.

One stone wall loomed up 620 feet. I saw guards with rifles perched on the corners, where day and night they watched for movement below, like eagles watching their prey. The run began, and I started jogging around the dirt path that circled the edges of the Yard, where only a few sprigs of grass had survived.

The prisoners ran faster than I did, although I was a runner then and could jog for hours. Was it because running was one of the few exercises they had to occupy their time? An inmate fell in beside me. He was clean-shaven and looked like someone I might have run with at Duke University, inside a much lower campus wall, in Durham, North Carolina.

I wanted to find out what he was in for, but Sing Sing was a prison for murderers, so I simply asked, "Where y'all from?"

Picking up on my accent, he said, "Where are you from?"

I was from nearby Sleepy Hollow but answered his true question: "It's a Georgia accent."

"I thought so."

"How'd you know?" I asked.

"Was on the chain gang in Georgia, recognize that accent anywhere." His voice turned bitter, perhaps at his memories.

Back then, prisoners were chained together or wore heavy balls around their ankles as they worked along the roads. If a prisoner tried to escape, tracking hounds were set loose. The guards who accompanied them might shoot first and answer questions later. I wondered how strong his hostility was and whether my life could be in imminent danger. Did he associate me with his Georgia experience?

Although he didn't make a move toward me, cold chills rose under my shirt. Then I realized it wasn't about his anger, but about my own sense of guilt.

We raised $3,000 for Sing Sing literacy, which would buy over three hundred books for the inmates. Whether I had this job or not seemed insignificant next to what reading would mean to these men.

The phrase for keeping inmates from coming back to prison is preventing recidivism. So when I felt down in the dumps, I'd stop and think how books bought with money we'd raised prevented inmate recidivism, and my spirits soared.

After the new cable TV company moved in, they requested that all newly acquired employees hand in their resignations on the following Monday. That Monday afternoon, the general manager called me into his office. This is it, I thought. He asked me a dozen questions about specific communities and the company's relationship with them. After about a half hour, he thanked me for bringing him up-to-date.

As I turned to leave, I said, "Oh, you forgot to take my resignation," and I handed it to him.

"Not you," he said, smiling and handing it back.

A few years later, Continental Cablevision acquired American Cablesystems, and the process began again. Perhaps the acquiring companies had heard I was a hard worker who would do whatever necessary for the job. Or perhaps they knew how fascinated I was being the liaison to dozens of communities with different lifestyles and personalities, unlike the sameness of the English, Scottish, and Irish Southerners I had grown up with in Georgia and Alabama.

Or maybe they realized I was following my design and doing a job I loved. All I do know is that each time I handed in my resignation to a new company as they had requested from all employees, they said, "Not you." So I worked in cable TV for four different companies spanning twenty-six years. Who could have dreamed that, when I stood on that special spot on the sidewalk in Griffin, Georgia, wishing over and over to go out into the world and do something?

HELLO, KITTY

Every day had felt like a birthday party with lighted candles when I was an interviewer on cable TV, scrambling away from the family underdog role of my childhood. It was a presidential election year and interviews were like adding presents to the celebration. I was to interview Kitty Dukakis, the wife of a presidential candidate. Among the usual questions, I had also written in my script book: What things will Mike do to help the cause of women? What would you like to accomplish in your First Lady role?

As it turned out, at the last minute I was given a script of approved topics by the Dukakis-for-President headquarters. Waiting with Kitty for the on-air signal, my mind wandered to thoughts she might have revealed, like the unruly ideas we all have.

But, in order not to cause trouble, I pitched a

softball: "What does Michael think are the most important things he will accomplish as president?" And, "What are his chances of winning the Democratic presidential nomination?"

As she began her polished responses, I thought, what am I accomplishing? I've spent eight years asking other people about their lives. I should move on—now!

Moms would be disappointed, no longer able to impress her bridge club with saying, "Guess who Emilie interviewed today?" I'd never chosen myself over Moms' approval before. Now I wanted to. Thank you, Kitty, for helping me reveal secrets of my own.

Kitty (she's still here?) said, "Michael would be a conciliator ..."

That was a good trait and a good answer, I thought, between my thoughts.

What would I do if I quit being on TV? I'd been talking about my negotiating skills with a friend. I'd negotiated my way out of numerous speeding tickets. And relatives had repeatedly told how my Texas grandfather Lorenzo negotiated buying a race horse while walking into Borger, Texas. The negotiating trait must be genetic.

Kitty, looking directly into the eye of the camera, said, "I hope all of you watching will vote for Michael in the primary!"

"Thank you, Kitty, and great success to you both!" I said warmly.

Still seated, we shook hands, our smiles frozen, waiting for the floor manager to give his you're off-the-air signal—a slit-your-throat gesture.

That afternoon, before I lost my nerve, I walked upstairs to talk with Dave, the regional vice president. I explained how just doing interviews every day made me feel like a parrot on a perch. I'd like to add to my job description, negotiating contracts, changes of ownership, and placing towers and dishes in residential neighborhoods.

Dave didn't hesitate to sign on. He'd be able to stay home with his young family, and I'd attend meetings as government relations director. Once I was telling a woman Supervisor two counties to the north that I'd come to their town meeting that night. Emilie, she laughed, you better get in your car now, we are two hours away, so I did.

One of my most satisfying times was when a new cable company was visiting and I needed to get town approval for the buyout to go through. To my horror, the elected officials turned me down. Somehow I found myself standing and going back to the podium saying, "Excuse me, I must have done a terrible job of making the case for this wonderful change. Then I gave every other reason I could think of in favor.

To this day, I haven't figured out if the board approved so they could go home that night, or because they appreciated chutzpah, or they had been in a similar fix themselves.

Kitty Dukakis, wife of Presidential candidate Mike Dukakis and Emilie on-the-air in Cablevision's Peekskill, New York studio.

JUST ASK FOR FOUR THINGS

It was an accident. Or maybe in my stars. Or Moms gave me bullseye advice. Perhaps it was all three of them, I'm not exactly sure.

At a party where food and poinsettias filled the room and neighbors chatted about snow blowers and which trains to New York City ran on time, a man in a white turtleneck, navy jacket, and khaki pants named Ferguson said, "Emilie, what's wrong? You seem so distracted."

I told him I had no idea what to ask for at my salary review the next day with Continental Cablevision, the new company.

Without hesitating, he said, "It's easy, ask for four things: stock in the company, a car, an MBA, and double the money you want."

"I can do that," I said, and didn't think about my review again until the next morning. I strode into the office of Al, the vice president. I could feel the yellow 3x5 card in my suit pocket with the four phrases written on it, just in case I got nervous and forgot my lines. Then, I could just pull it out and read it, although I didn't think I'd have to since as Ferguson had said, "It's easy."

"What do you have in mind for next year?" Al asked. What a perfect lead-in, but I took a breath, trying not to appear eager, and I asked for the four items on the card.

Al explained that the owner, Steve Dodge, decided who received stock in the company. Now I know who to be nice to, I was thinking. Actually, I believe I said it out loud. Al laughed.

About the car, he replied that people on call with a beeper get a car. "Do you want one?" I declined.

My third suggestion, that I get an MBA, was a negotiating ploy, so that when we got to the salary discussion, he would up the ante.

But his third answer stunned me. "An MBA, what a great idea. It'll help you negotiate with the Pomona bankers."

He and I had recently discussed cable TV contract terms with five male elected officials in Rockland County, bankers who talked about what our ROI was in their village, and asked did we scorch the earth so other companies wouldn't come in.

"I, well, um, thank you for offering me to pay for my MBA," I said.

The last negotiating point was my salary, and he suggested more money than I had anticipated. We shook hands and parted.

An MBA? I pictured men in tweed jackets with patches on the elbows with an MBA diploma on their walls, or men with slicked-back hair à la Wall Street and wearing silk suits as they commuted downtown in New York City. Did a mother of three children with a full-time job belong in their austere company?

Perplexed over what was the right decision, I drove home thinking of nothing else. Actually, I don't remember driving home or even putting the car key in the ignition. So before I even took my coat off, I called Moms in Alabama for advice.

"The new company offered me an MBA." In sixty seconds I elaborated on the terms of the deal. "What do you think?"

"Toots, what exactly is your question?"

Ding. Her three-minute timer went off, and a buzz filled the air between Alabama and New York. Without another word, we both hung up.

In two years I had my MBA, and shortly thereafter I was offered a job as the general manager of a cable TV system of mostly male technicians. Now, when financially inclined officials asked me, "What's your cash cow?" I knew what to say.

And as strange as it seems, those three letters on a piece of paper made others think I could do magic. And right or wrong, I believed it too.

ASK HIGH, DROP LOW,
BE ABLE TO WALK AWAY

I was restlessly flipping the pages of an airline magazine while on a long flight from New York to California when I noticed a full page ad: Karrass: Negotiation Made Easy, $1500.

Since I knew you learn as much from fellow participants as you do from the instructor, I called Karrass headquarters to find out where the most talented students might be. "Los Angeles and New York City," an employee said. Since New York City was only a train, not a plane, ride away, I signed up for a two-day workshop at the Sheraton Hotel. The cable company agreed to pay—the easiest negotiation I was to have over the next ten years.

On the first morning, I laid out my pink suit and took a shower. Dick, who daily commuted the twenty miles to New York City from Sleepy Hollow, called in to me, "The schedule has changed and you have fifteen minutes to get to the station." I flew out the door with wet hair hanging down my neck and my makeup stuffed in my briefcase.

I knew it was verboten to talk on a commuter train, but I never heard Dick say anything about not putting on makeup. So I did. Since my hair is straight, drip dry was fine. Less attractive were the water spots on my suit's shoulders.

Arriving barely ahead of schedule, I asked a bellman if he had a pen or pencil since I had raced out without either.

After fumbling in his many pockets, he said, "I'll find one and bring it up to you."

"Don't you want my name?"

"No, I'll be able to recognize you."He smiled so broadly, his gums showed.

I walked up to the second floor and peeked into a room filled with men in dark suits, each and every one of which looked tailor-made. I crept in. There were no other women in the room, which was fine with me. I took a seat near the front, next to a fellow who said he was a fur trader from Canada. He, it turned out, would be my negotiating opponent.

As the facilitator was clearing his throat to commence the program, the bellman knocked, getting everyone's attention, and said in a loud voice, "Where's the little lady who needs a pencil?"

I was mortified and thought I detected a few smirks. Fortunately, the pencil had an eraser, since I knew I'd make lots of mistakes.

"Your first exercise," said Jim, the facilitator, "will be to negotiate with your seatmate. I'll give each of you a piece of paper with the name of the item over which you'll bargain."

My slip read, "You have a truck to sell that barely runs (just like my lima-bean-colored Ford) but it's guaranteed to arrive at its destination."

Unbeknownst to me, Larry's piece of paper said, "You have a truck-size load of rotting fruit you must get to market today or you'll lose your entire investment."

Jim said that sellers should get $500 or as close to that as possible. "Start!"

I asked Larry for $1,000, thinking he would probably want to split the deal and I'd get my $500. Larry proposed to pay half, $500, so still having time I asked him for $750, again halfway back. The buzzer went off.

Not having consummated a deal, I quickly whispered to Larry, "Tell you what, just so we both feel good about this, how about $650?"

He agreed, smiling, but his smile didn't last long.

My $650 turned out to be the highest amount anyone got for the truck. "Larry," asked Jim, "what was your thinking process working?"

"I'd rather not say," Larry mumbled.

Silence from Larry. Silence from Jim. Silence from the participants, shifting, ill at ease. Larry finally said, "I felt sorry for her. She seemed rather helpless. I guess...I let my guard down."

Larry didn't come back the second day. Perhaps never let sympathy get in the way of making a good deal was all he needed to know. Other participants now treated me with respect and seemed to want to try their hand at negotiating with me. They were pros and not reluctant to share their best ideas. And we who stayed learned the importance of developing a good relationship with our opponents.

These negotiating skills fit every situation I came across over the next fifteen years. I didn't need to be sophisticated, as I was trying so hard to be. I just needed to know these four pillars of negotiating:

- Ask high, then come down a little.
- Give something to make the other person feel good.
- Always be your truthful self.
- Don't be afraid to walk away. If you're not willing to walk away, you can't really negotiate.

SING SING II

I thought the run for literacy was the end of my Sing Sing prisoner adventures, but it wasn't. About a year later, a prisoner escaped from Sing Sing in the false bottom of a laundry truck, then walked five miles down the railroad tracks along the Hudson River to our small village. At shallow points in the river, he entered the water so hounds would lose his scent. Anyone having grown up in the south, and probably any prisoner, would know to do that. When he arrived in our heavily wooded neighborhood near Sleepy Hollow Manor, he waded ashore looking for a place to hide.

I remember it was a cold December night, a Thursday, and I had a paper due for my MBA class the next day. Writing was going slowly, so I said to Dick and the girls at supper, "Do not disturb me for any reason. Nothing is more important than turning in my paper on time."

"Even if there's an earthquake?" Kristiana, who was ten, asked.

"That or worse!" I said emphatically.

A few hours later, a helicopter with a searchlight flew back and forth around our neighborhood, lighting up our small block and shining in my window. Steadfast to my studies—hard for inquisitive me—I refused to look out.

At 9:00 p.m. our doorbell rang. I could barely hear a policeman tell Dick he was checking homes since the escaped convict had been tracked to our neighborhood. Dick assured him we were fine.

Distracted, I thought of our blue VW bus parked in the driveway and how it would be a perfect place to hide. I called down without leaving my study room, "Please lock the bus."

According to radio reports, the escaped prisoner was found sleeping in a small station wagon two blocks away, when police noticed steam on its windows.

Susie said, "If he had been in our huge VW van, he might not have been caught." Not to mention how surprised Dick would have been when he opened the van door to go to the train station in the morning.

When I told my MBA professor that this report might not be my best effort and why, he said my excuse was the best he'd heard in twenty years. He might even give me extra points for creativity.

But he didn't.

I wished the escapee could have spent his energy learning to read with the books American Cablesystems funded from the literacy run. Who knows? He might have been granted parole and stayed out of prison.

Sing Sing Prison, Circa 1920

I'M ESSENTIAL, WHAT ABOUT YOU?

A Saturday blizzard dumped eighteen inches of snow on New York State, making roads icy and impassible. Early Sunday morning, Governor Mario Cuomo proclaimed that all nonessential drivers were to stay at home. Roads needed to be kept open for snow removal and emergency vehicles.

I told Dick I would never accept being called nonessential. Mario couldn't be talking about me. I felt I'd always done essential work—as a second-grade teacher, a mother, and now as program director for McLean Cable. I kept locals informed about what was going on; and cable was a lifeline for the elderly and the ailing who couldn't venture out, especially during a storm.

Thinking it over reinforced my confidence that my role in cable TV was important. Not that I had ever doubted it. And to any local police officer who might be inclined to stop my car and say, "Nonessential," I was ready to make an in-your-face justification for my trip to the station—putting the Big Game on the air. Maybe the officer himself had played in the game years before and would give me an escort.

There was a complication. Growing up in Georgia and Alabama, where we rarely had snow, meant I wasn't a skilled driver in this kind of weather. To tell the truth, I was terrible.

Rather than taking the car, with my head held high, I trudged down our driveway wearing snow boots and a faux-fur trapper hat, thinking I'd walk the two miles into town.

In the stillness, I listened to the crunch of my boots on the snow. It was otherwise silent. No cars, no birds, and no people. Best of all to me was making the first tracks. Did the first person to make tracks on the moon feel like that—but in a global way?

Interrupting my reverie was a happy sight, a neighbor in a car with four-wheel drive backing out of his driveway. He was probably in a hurry to get cinnamon buns at Alters Bakery on Cortlandt Street before they sold out. People in the village would surely have walked there as soon as it opened at seven.

Having grown up in a small town in the South where everyone was neighborly, I raised my thumb. He hesitantly rolled down his window in the bitter cold, probably not wanting to chill his cozy car. Or maybe my trapper hat had scared him into thinking, There goes the neighborhood; or he didn't want anyone to see me, which might make real estate prices plummet.

I didn't know if he was going in my direction anyway, but he let me off at the cable TV station. I thanked him profusely for the lift. Still in a rush, he grunted, "Anytime."

I'd promoted the game for weeks, publicizing it everywhere. We had been running a streamer twenty-four hours a day on the channel. The football game was between arch rivals, the Sleepy Hollow High School Headless Horsemen and the neighboring Ossining High School Indians. Almost everyone who went to the game would want to watch the rerun. On top of that, I'd taught our camera crews to pan the crowd at timeouts and choose two Fans of the Week. Each fan got a T-shirt that read, "I saw you on Channel 26—Watch It!" This pulled in an even bigger viewership.

I could picture whole families gathered in living rooms in the Tarrytowns, wearing the school colors, red and black, and sitting in front of boxy TVs that inevitably sat on wooden stands. Chances were they'd be eating chicken fingers, chips and dip, and passing around a huge bowl of Jiffy Pop. I could see the drizzle of butter that would drip on their pants or the patterned rug. How could I possibly let these people down?

I cued up the two-hour videotape and pushed play.

As I was going out the door, George, the cable TV general manager, startled me by coming in. He had driven his car with its jumbo snow tires and said he was dumbfounded that I was there. Then he stood still on the stoop for a minute and said, "Actually, I'm not surprised at all." George went inside to do … exactly what, I'm not sure. Was he truly an essential driver that day? I wondered?

The next morning at Bella's Restaurant on Broadway, the breakfast place of choice for miles around, the game would be rehashed. No one would think to say it was great that Emilie of McLean Cable had hitchhiked in and put the game on during a blizzard. But I knew my getting the game on was essential, and that was comfort enough for me.

CODE WORDS

In only a few syllables, code words can tell an entire story. And they do it with the warmth of memories shared. Best of all to me, a lone word is so spare, it doesn't give a spouse or relative time to say, "You've told me that before."

CHAMONIX

It was bitterly cold in the mountains of Chamonix, France, the frost edging up the outside wall and into the hotel where we were to spend the night after a day of trekking. In the dining room, we kept our gloves on, buttoned our coats, and pulled our hats down as far as they would go. We shivered our way through reading the menu, wrapped in thoughts of hypothermia and pneumonia.

Our entire group ordered the potato, garlic, and

mushroom soup, hoping it would stay warm enough to thaw us out. To our amazement, it arrived steaming hot and stayed hot, despite the frigid condition of the room. When I asked the waiter how that could be, he said, "We always heat the bowls."

Every winter since, I heat plates and soup bowls prior to serving anything I want to stay hot.

"Where are the dishes?" Dick asks.

"Chamonix," I reply, and he goes straight to the microwave.

GALVESTON

Daddy told me a story about a night when lightning, thunder, and pounding rain lashed the cowboy and oil towns of the Texas Panhandle. "Flooding on the roads is anticipated," the weatherwoman predicted on the five o'clock news while six members of the Smith family lounged in their modest living room trying to decide what to do about dinner.

"We could drive to Galveston to that new restaurant," said Juanita, my dad's sister. "The weather is bad, it's an hour away, and I haven't heard any rave reviews, but no one would have to cook."

"I guess that would be okay," said Daddy's mother, Molly.

"I'd go along with that," his father Lorenzo echoed.

The three other family members nodded in agreement, so they piled into the sedan and drove through the pounding rain. They were squashed together and the trip took much longer than anticipated.

"We had a miserable ride in the rain," Daddy said, "and a flavorless but expensive dinner." The waitress had been grouchy, the ride back worse than the ride over, and nobody said much.

Once home, Grandpa told them that he hadn't really wanted to go all the way to Galveston in the first place, "but I didn't want to disappoint you."

Grandmother Molly chimed in, "And I didn't want to be a spoilsport."

Oldest brother Ralph said, "I guess none of us wanted to go."

They decided that next time they should all speak up.

Two generations later, the code word continues. When family members are about to make a decision, invariably someone asks in a voice filled with dread, "Is this going to be a trip to Galveston?"

NEXT PLAY

Duke was a mixed bag of experiences when I transferred there as a junior. But when I became an alumna, Basketball Coach K. taught me a new code word. In an interview with the *Durham Herald*, he told a reporter that when he needed to encourage his players, he yelled, "Next play!" It meant move past the negatives and concentrate *only* on the next bit of action.

I read that over breakfast on a visit to Janet's house. I put down the paper and thought of things I needed to leave behind, peeves against my mother, annoyance that my editor takes out good stories, and that I couldn't keep my weight steady at 145. The list goes on.

A few nights later when I sat in Cameron indoor arena watching a Duke basketball game, Coach K. did call out "Next play!" The words echoed over the shiny hardwood floor and the bleachers, before bouncing off the steel rafters and settling over players and spectators like a patchwork quilt of pieced-together advice.

Before the shot clock could tick off another second, I could almost see players throw off negative thoughts as they rallied round each other and focused on their task. Their bewildered opponents, who had been substantially ahead, lost a game that had seemed already chalked in their column.

Finally, after years of trying to figure out exactly what was the Duke secret of winning against all odds, it was as clear to me as the water I had drunk from the north-end water fountain. Now, if something isn't going well, I whisper to myself. *Next play* and move on.

ALWAYS LOOK BACK

My next code word is actually three words: Always Look Back.

I was working for a startup cable TV channel, Cable

News Network, CNN, in 1981. Our assignment was to go to three crossroads of the United States—White Plains, Kansas City, and San Diego—to make commercials for the channel.

My job was to choose photogenic people at a mall, stop them, and tell them they were perfect to do a commercial for CNN. If they agreed, I'd ask them to say in their own words why it was important for everyone to watch the network. Then I'd get them to sign a release that had been carefully written and vetted by CNN's legal department.

When we arrived at the San Diego airport for the final set of tapings, I found a pay phone so I could call home and check up on Dick and Kristi. As I began the call, Garrett, the director, rushed up and said, "Come quick, our van is here." He told me to go to the arrivals sign outside as soon as I could.

"Good-bye, feed her some vegetables, not just pizza," I said to Dick, hoping the production van hadn't been towed. I raced outside without looking back, breaking a rule I'd adhered to since the girls were little—Always Look Back.

As I started to unpack at the hotel, I realized I had left the authorization forms on the shelf of the pay phone. All our work in New York and Kansas City would be worthless if I didn't find the releases.

I immediately called the airport manager, who understood the situation and had an employee race to my pay phone. After what seemed to be eternity, he told me he had the forms. I jumped in a cab and, when I arrived at the airport, all but ran to his office.

I thanked him profusely for finding the forms. "We've all done something similar," he said graciously, and seemed to be thinking about his own moment.

On the way back to the hotel, I thought that if I had only looked back, I could have been sipping my second pinot noir at the hotel bar with the crew.

Ever since that day, as we start out on a family trip together, my offspring whisper to each other, "Three, two, one. It's time for Mom to tell us to look back for what we've left behind."

I always say it, and forgotten items are remembered just in the nick of time. I don't expect my children, or anyone else, to remember and thank me, but I hope they'll learn, as I did, that hard-earned wisdom can be dispatched in just a handful of words.

GRUDGES BE GONE

When I harbor a grudge after getting my feelings hurt, to shake it free I concentrate on the Buddhist monks' story.

One spring afternoon, wearing their saffron-colored robes, while walking, talking, and observing nature, an elder and a young monk arrived at a rushing river.

A woman in pungent rags approached and said to the elder monk, "Please, sir, would you give me a ride on your back across the river? My child is sick and I have medicine."

The younger monk said to the elder, "But sir, monks are not supposed to touch women."

"Would it not be worse to leave the woman stranded here, with her child sick at home?" said the elder. He told the woman to hop on his back. "Let's go quickly."

After struggling against the current with the additional weight, the old monk let the woman down gently on the other side. Without looking back or expressing thanks, the woman shuffled off down the dusty road toward her home in the village.

The two monks trudged on until they arrived at their destination. As they were about to part, the young monk turned and chastised his elder. "Father, why did you carry that woman? You broke our rules, and you could have perished. And she wasn't even grateful."

"The older monk said, "I set down the woman, her troubles, and my transgressions when I reached this side of the river. I am free. Why are you still carrying the burden?"

To rid myself of a grudge, I think about the monk story and say to myself, "I've crossed the river. Why am I still carrying the burden?" And I imagine myself throwing scruffy stuff on the ground, shaking my shoulders free, and walking away. Bizarre as it seems, it usually works.

PAPER ROUTE

Susie wanted a stereo so she could play Stevie Wonder songs blasting in her room.

"Mom, would you buy me one?"

"Why don't you get a paper route and *buy it yourself,* like you learned in Montessori? When I was a girl…"

"Oh, never mind," she said.

Dick, Susie and I drove our VW bus with the Grateful Dead sticker to the Tarrytown Daily News.

You may think it strange for me to have that sticker on the car I drove to work every day. But, I had proclaimed to the girls that people who had Grateful Dead stickers on their vehicles were certified pot heads. Then, as I was going into the grocery, the girls declined, saying they had some serious shopping to do.

When I came out, the sticker was stuck on, and they were sitting in the car pretending to look out the windows at something fascinating. I was going to scrape the sticker off that week, but before I could get around to it, the young guys at the cable office where I worked as the manager said, "I didn't know you liked the Grateful Dead, too!" They gave me an accepting sort of look, so I left the sticker on.

When we arrived at the newspaper front office in Tarrytown, they sent us to the warehouse.

"I wanna be a newspaper girl," Susie said to the muscular man in blue jeans and a plaid shirt.

"Oof," he grunted as he picked up a huge bundle of

papers and plopped it down on the dusty bed of a truck.

"How old are ya?" he asked.

"Eleven."

"Gotta be twelve."

"I really want this job and I'll be good at it," Susie said. "You'll be glad you hired me."

"Could put it in your Pop's name," the man said, as he scratched his ear and relented.

"Okay-y-y." Dick said. Family members, and now the warehouse man knew, Susie could be persuasive, bordering on relentless, and it was easier to give in if the situation wasn't life threatening.

A few days later, Susie, two of the three neighboring triplets Larry and Kevin, and her best friend Katie began delivering papers to our winding route of homes in Sleepy Hollow Manor. Susie tallied the numbers in a ledger, collected the payments, and soon enough bought herself a stereo and speakers.

When she was sick or there was a blizzard, Dick and I delivered her papers. He drove, and I threw the folded papers out the passenger window, making a game of trying to hit the front porch – harder to do than it seems. Susie even delivered them from the car with Dick when there was an escaped convict in the neighborhood.

And, twenty-five years later, when the girls flew home to help Dick and me with our moving sale, Susie gave the stereo to a teenager from the inner village. He didn't care that this model had been usurped by smaller, hipper equipment.

"Mom," Susie said, "he wanted it as much as I had back then, but *he* didn't have to work for it."

"In this case, that's okay, don't you think?"

Susie nodded.

As our family stood in front of the stone wall for the last time, watching the stereo equipment being loaded into a scratched and dented truck, we felt as if an era had ended, and indeed it had.

And that is how *paper route"* became the code words for *why don't you do it yourself?*

SPAIN—COMPRENDEZ ALTO?

Our plane lifted off in the evening mist from JFK, where lights lining the edges of the runway twinkled like fireflies. Actually, even a muddy ditch would have looked beautiful to me at that moment.

After we boarded, Dick and I took our seats and tried to look nonchalant. We were escapees from Brooklyn Heights, having recently hugged and kissed our two daughters good-bye—Amy, three, and Susie, two. We were going to Europe, hoping their northern and southern grandmas, who'd be caring for them, would think we were too far away to call.

The grandmas had concocted the idea of sending Dick and me away for a month, possibly thinking we might not make it otherwise.

Caroline, Dick's mother, would be in charge of meals (mostly frozen Stouffers) and sightseeing (mostly New York City museums). Esther, my mother, would be in charge of the rest. We couldn't believe how kind they were being to take this project on.

Madrid was our first stop, but it could have been Milwaukee or Miami or even Marietta. We would have been equally excited.

It was late when we checked into our hotel between the Bodega and the Pharmacia on the outskirts of the Spanish capitol. Not wanting to waste a moment, since we were in a foreign country and starved, we went to a nearby restaurant. Carved wooden chairs and bright embroidered tablecloths screamed Buenos Dias. If that didn't tell us we were in Spain, waiters in black bullfighter-type outfits standing at attention did.

When we ordered, Dick pointed to an item on the menu written entirely in Spanish.

"Tostados, por favor." Dick's accent was impeccable since he had studied Spanish in high school.

"Honey," I said, "I think that means just toast." But what did I know, after only one year of Spanish at the University of Miami?

"No, look down here," he said, and pointed at something on the menu.

I was in love and on a romantic getaway, so I didn't look, much less argue. I ordered paella, which I knew was rice and tomatoes and shrimp mixed together with spices, a classic Spanish dish that even I had heard about.

The waiters came out and with ceremony placed my entree lovingly in front of me. The two of them lifted high the silver-domed warming cover. Strange, the cover didn't look that heavy, but that must be the way things are served in Spain.

Then they stood with big smiles beside Dick's place, lifting off a second dome with even greater gusto.

I tried not to laugh, honestly, but there winking up like square eyes were not one but two pieces of pale brown toast, cooked to perfection.

"Olé," the waiters said, as if they were indeed bullfighters.

Dick recovered quickly, choosing something entirely different. I don't remember what it was, but this time it was under entrées. Probably to save face, he ordered Baked Alaska for dessert—a huge platter of meringue, ice cream, and rum which they set on fire, so dramatic and expensive. It was the most romantic finish to a meal I could remember.

Dick must have left a gigante tip because the bullfighters, I mean waiters, began discussing with us what we should do the next day. Mostly through pantomime, they recommended, for such a dramatic couple, the Gran Prix car race. We said, "Si, si," and decided we'd go.

What I was thinking as we walked back to the hotel was, why hadn't I bought a pocket dictionary of English/Spanish with expressions that I could thumb through and use? I did buy one the next day, even though it was backward for me, with Spanish translated to English in the front and English to Spanish in back.

We drove on mostly dirt roads before we came to the Gran Prix, which seemed to encourage reckless driving. Brightly painted cars zoomed around under the blazing sun. When the black car won, spectators with winning tickets tossed their hats into the air, and those who had lost tossed their betting slips into the dirt. Some things are universal.

As I drove back to the hotel, locals careened around each other in Gran Prix style—passing on the shoulders of the road, honking, and cutting in and out as if they too were in a racing ring. Some appeared on our rear bumper and then jerked away at the last moment.

"Where are the cops?" I asked Dick as I drove along at a normal speed.

"I think you'll see one right behind you, the one with the flashing lights," he said.

The Spanish policeman who got out and stood beside my window said, "Senorita, comprendez alto?"

I said, "No, sir, I don't speak Spanish. I'm from the United States."

"Alto, alto!" He raised his voice a little. Well, maybe a lot.

Meekly I said, "No comprendez."

Now, since I had spoken Spanish to him, he spoke

English to me.

"It means stop!" And he pointed to what must have been a Spanish stop sign.

How was I supposed to know stop when I saw alto hand painted on a piece of metal? The sign wasn't red. It wasn't a hexagon. It didn't say Stop, just Alto.

I turned pale.

"Alto esta stop! Comprendez? Vamos! Vamos!" The policeman, whose face was now rojo, waved me on with his hands.

"Si, senor, alto. Adios!" I said, waving.

At least the policeman didn't say stupido. Neither did Dick. But I knew what they were thinking. But, toast anyone?

France—A Strike in Paris

It was time to move on to our next stop, the romantic lights of enchanting Paris.

It was an ordinary day until the Air France ticket agent told us they could fly us into Paris, but not out. There was a strike. We asked him how long he thought the strike might last. "Je ne sais pas." I don't know, he had said, and shrugged. I reassured the airline employee that he shouldn't worry about us. We lived in New York City, home of numerous strikes. We New Yorkers—I considered myself a local now—knew just what to do.

"Madam, the strike is huge," he said.

I would later regret that I insisted on traveling despite his warnings, and would wish I could inhale those words back into my mouth and swallow them whole. In that very moment, however, I was pleased to have convinced the agent to print our plane tickets, even if it was against his better judgment. I imagine I strutted a little as we walked onto the tarmac to board our plane, which was almost empty. The month of May must be off-season, I thought.

On the taxi ride from Orly airport to our rental in a home on the Left Bank, I read the guidebook that said students lived and congregated in this section. Thinking of the happy students in Auburn where I grew up, I decided this was surely the safest place to be. With our two children at home, I hadn't had much time to pay attention to the anti-Vietnam War movement going on in France and much of Europe.

As the taxi drove along, we noticed that museums, public buildings, and even stores were closed. It must be a holiday. Next I saw policemen stationed on every corner in riot gear. The norm for French cities, I assumed.

Approaching the Left Bank, I was alarmed to see overturned cars and students shouting in the streets. When we got to our landlady's house, she was surprised to see us. I began to realize we had miscalculated.

"Dick, do something," I said, even though I was the one who'd insisted we come to Paris and ignore the strike. Surely this fell in the category of things a man should handle—getting us out of town during a crippling strike in Paris. Dick said he'd try to find us a way to escape, that he would go to the train station and buy us two tickets to anywhere.

The next morning, after croissants of course, Dick

left on his mission. The streets were filled with an obstacle course of broken furniture, bottles, and smoldering cars. The smell of burnt rubber hung in the air. Dick was gone so long, it gave me plenty of time to imagine what terrible things might be happening.

After what seemed an eternity, Dick returned. He said the train station had been padlocked, encased in barbed wire, and surrounded by pieces of furniture stacked five layers high, creating an impenetrable barrier. Abandoned trains stood on the rails, which he said reminded him of a toy set waiting for Christmas—or in this case, until the strike was over.

Then he said he had what he thought might be good news. A man standing in the outer shadows of the station had said he could get us out. The stranger had explained we could ride in his jitney van, leaving the train station at 6:00 p.m. on Friday. It would take us to the French/German border in Salzburg. Dick had been relieved to hear that. Then the man had asked him to pay the full amount for the trip, in cash, on the spot. Dick, seeing no other options, took a chance and gave the Frenchman francs we had fortunately bought at the airport.

"You gave a stranger money?" I asked. I was sure the man would not be there when the time came. Why would he bother? I wanted to call Dick a rube, but we were on our romantic getaway together, so I kept quiet, which was hard for me to do.

On Friday before six, Dick and I hurried to the

barricaded train station with our suitcases, mine being the white Samsonite I'd bought in Miami when my blue cardboard one fell apart. Parked in front of the boarded-up train station was a dirty beat-up Peugeot van with the driver. Nothing had ever looked so beautiful.

"Vite, vite." Quick, quick, he whispered, and kept glancing around as we piled aboard. Six others, all Americans, were already seated. The driver closed the door, and we headed out into total darkness. The electricity had been cut by students. There was no moon.

After an hour on the winding road, a suitcase fell from the rack on top of the van. "Stop!" we passengers yelled. The driver told us we didn't have time to pick up the suitcase, that we'd miss our train. As we were protesting, the owner of the errant case ran out, brought the bag inside, and held it on her lap.

A few hours later, the van stopped at a pitch-black place in the road. This is it, I thought. We'll be robbed and killed. Or we'll be abandoned, and who knows what would happen then. I wished I'd paid more attention in French class so I'd be able to negotiate with our kidnappers.

We were told to run straight ahead to the train. We ran on faith, as if our lives depended on it. There wasn't anything else we could do. Our day would surely feel familiar to an immigrant trying to cross a border at night. Had we all felt the same, optimistic that things would turn out all right while not really knowing? Keeping hope while awaiting our fate?

Above the trees ahead were bright lights. We ran a hundred yards until we came to a train with steam coming from its engine, filling the night with smoke.

We rushed onto the train seemingly seconds before it pulled away from the station. Dick and I sank down on the yellow leather benches of a glass-doored compartment.

"Whew," we said.

But we shouldn't have, because just then a conductor in a military-looking uniform and boots up to his knees slid open the door and clicked his heels together. Clack.

In German, he asked for our tickets. Since we had no tickets, he asked more loudly, for our passports. Dick, of course, immediately pulled his passport out of his jacket pocket. I, of course, fumbled around in my pocketbook, finding makeup and gum and … Ah, here it is, and I handed it to the man with the knee boots. After what seemed to be an eternity, he sold us tickets, clicked his heels together, and moved forward. Soon enough the train and Dick and I moved forward as well. We hugged each other and I thought how we had worked as a team.

"We may not have seen the bright lights of Paris," I said, "but we are about to see the bright lights of Germany."

We looked at each other, "Germany?"

Future vacations have continued to be self-guided treks in Europe among friends, L to R: Warren, Dick, Emilie, Judy, Betty, Tony, Clyde and Don.

MA HAD A GIFT

Emilie Bubolz, my Wisconsin grandmother whom we called Ma, had the ability to sense things she couldn't have known about. She passed this gift down with no clear pattern of inheritance. Some descendants never experienced this lucky—or unlucky—trait.

Family legend has it that one night Ma woke up with the terrible knowledge that one of her children was on the verge of passing over. It is said that she knelt on the braided rug, placed her folded hands on the black quilt with pink roses, and asked the Lord to have mercy on Richard, one of her thirteen children.

Moments later the special ring on the party line jangled. A caller said that Richard, away at college, had been injured in a car accident. They didn't know whether he would survive. Ma and Dad expected the worst. No one knows if Ma made a pact with God to be a faithful servant if Richard lived. We do know that for the rest of her life, Ma prayed every morning and read the Bible every night. Richard survived, continued his education, and became a surgeon.

Decades later, a couple Dick and I met in New Hampshire expressed surprise that we were going to hike the Dolomites of Italy. We thought they were being prejudicial because we were older than they, even though we told them we had been hiking for years in the mountains of Europe. They were still skeptical, given the difficulty of the trek.

A few weeks later, Dick and I and our hiking buddies from California and London trekked in the Dolomites. We hiked on narrow, winding paths of tiny loose rocks near the edges of cliffs. It was breathtakingly steep, and there was nothing between us and the sea. To find our way, we spotted rocks painted with red blazes that pointed out the correct path around the craggy mountains shown on our maps. We had no actual guide, since orienteering was as important to this group as was the climb. We rarely asked for current information at the overnight refugio where we stayed. On this morning, we should have done so.

We were walking briskly, until Clyde, in the lead, called back to us, agitated. There had been a rock slide and stones of all sizes now blocked our way. Dick and Warren followed a popular emergency procedure and dropped to the ground, keeping their centers of gravity low. They crawled on their bellies back to safety, their arms and legs becoming scratched and bloody. "Don't try it," they called to me.

I tried to retreat, but with each step slipped down a little. My poles wouldn't grip, and there were no bushes to grab if I continued sliding to the sea, twenty stories below.

Surefooted Warren came back and asked me to hand him my back pole, while I balanced with both feet on the front one. He alternated jabbing the poles into hard ground as we made our way back toward safety—until he planted the pole for the fifth time. I felt frozen in place and couldn't make myself move.

"What's wrong?" he asked.

"A feeling of doom."

"I'll try a new spot," Warren said, and without hesitation he wrenched the offending pole out and chose a new spot at random. I'll never know if my feelings were accurate, but I survived, and inside I'm aware of their truth.

Back in North Carolina, Amy was studying the night before her master's degree exam in Russian at Duke. She put the dozen books she was reviewing on the floor, shut off the light, and crawled into bed. No sooner did she lie down than she heard in her head, Get up and read the chapter on Russian folk tales. Although it was already the middle of the night, she turned the light back on, read the section, and drifted back to sleep. The next day there were three questions on her exam. The middle one was to write an essay about Russian folk tales.

Amy's son, Nick, was eight when he first exhibited ESP.

"Let's surprise Daddy at the mall," he said.

"He's at work," Amy said.

"Daddy really is at the mall," Nick said.

Amy called Joe to see how he was doing. He worked as an executive chef and at this time would be serving food at a corporate headquarters. When he told her he was at the mall buying new clogs because a strap was broken, she felt confused for a second, and then knew.

Amy thinks Nick may have gotten a double dose of this sixth sense, since his great-great-grandmother on his father's side was a healer in the mountains of Italy. Relatives report that locals would hike all the way up the mountain to get a cure for their ailments from her.

Amy and Joe listen to Nick's suggestions as if they are the most natural thing in the world, just as Ma and Dad's sons Gordon and George had listened to Ma in Wisconsin when she counseled them. In the family history, *Father Julius, Mother Emilie,* George wrote, "Ma has strong intuition—perceiving without using reasoning."

When I'm going out of the house, perhaps on a trip, I sometimes get instructions in my head, such as take pliers, or a particular book, or a second pair of shoes. I don't argue with the voice anymore, I just follow instructions. Inevitably someone will say, "I know this is a weird question, but does anyone have a pair of pliers?" Or my first pair of shoes get sopping wet and miraculously, I'm ready with a second pair.

I tell our grandchildren, "Trust your instincts. They might prove true and people will think you're a genius. And if your instincts don't turn out to be true, what harm is done?"

Ma would like these sayings, I'm sure of that.

GEORGIA AND NEW YORK CITY—
OLD TIMEY GAS STATION

Closer to home, in MOMA, the Museum of Modern Art on Fifty-Third Street and Fifth Avenue in New York City, nothing is too bizarre to appear on exhibit.

On a visit in 2013, I saw Edward Hopper's original painting of an old-fashioned gas station, similar to those found in the country in Georgia when I lived there. In the painting, a gas station attendant wearing black pants, a long-sleeved shirt, and a tie puts the gas pump handle back into its holder. Three red gasoline pumps with round glass lights on top light up the station in the approaching dusk. Surely, the Mobilgas sign with a flying red horse insignia catches the eye of anyone traveling this rural back road. The painting took my breath away.

I'd been to a gas station just like this one in Georgia

in 1945. My gas station attendant, however, wore a khaki workman's shirt and pants with a few grease spots here and there. Moms had just said to Daddy, "Why are we stopping here? This gas is way too expensive and you've taken us out of the way."

"I want the kids to see this station, there're not many left," Daddy said. He embraced historical memorabilia of all kinds, so we knew it was futile to protest. Groaning, we dutifully climbed out of the backseat of the navy Buick to take it all in, accompanied by the scraping sound of metal on metal from the out-of-alignment door.

Our gas station attendant filled the tank with regular, punched open a can of oil with a metal spout, poured it into the car's crank case, and refilled our radiator's emergency water jug. We gazed at it all briefly, not appreciating that these sights would soon disappear.

Standing in the museum in New York City, nostalgia filled me, as the gas had our tank, mixed with regret that I hadn't appreciated that earlier gas-station moment. I silently thanked Edward Hopper, the artist who in 1940 captured in oil paint on linen this rural event, and Daddy who was so thoughtful.

THE MORNING I SET OFF
AIRPORT SECURITY ALARMS

On the few occasions when I feel self-important and really smart, I remember the day I set off the alarms in airport security at JFK, and it jolts me back to reality.

It was a particularly dreary day around 4:30 a.m. when we started from home to go the airport. Believing that bright colors improve one's humor, I decided red would cheer up Dick and me, and perhaps everyone in the airport. I pulled on my red dress with four zippers and seven snaps, grabbed my carry-on suitcase, and we headed out on an empty road.

But let me go back just a little. The fashion of that particular month, according to Bill Cunningham of the New York Times, was literally a snappy dress with zippers. Completing the ensemble were metal studs that could be worn open or shut all the way down the front. Bill had declared buttons déclassé.

Our flight was an early one, leaving at 6:30, which means the tickets sell for a much cheaper rate. They were arranged by Dick, who enjoys a bargain almost as much as a trip. We were headed toward Kristiana and Greg's house in Las Vegas. Everything was going according to schedule, actually ahead of time. I'd even have a chance to get an iced coffee and a frosted cinnamon bun. I hoped that Dick wouldn't delay us going through security since he was often pulled aside and searched. On the other hand, they always waved me through. Perhaps being a blond helped.

We snaked forward in long lines until we finally reached security screening. I put my carry-on bag on the conveyor belt, took off my jacket and shoes, and strolled under the X-ray arches in a sleep-deprived trance.

So many squeals and beeps and bells went off, I thought I'd been transported straight to a gambling casino and that my slot machine hit pay dirt. The man in front of the security X-ray machine, who had a stern look that said everyone is a criminal, furrowed his brow until the frown lines in his forehead were as deep as if they'd be plowed by a mule in Alabama.

"Step over here," he said to me.

Uh-oh. I was in real trouble, but what had I done?

"Ma'am, lookit thuh screen. That's youse."

"That's me?" My good grammar—That is I—that Moms had drilled into my head must have been scared away.

The inspector said there were so many lighted dots, he didn't know where to start to look for dangerous weapons.

The metal zippers and snaps being lighted I could understand, but I noticed that all my underwear was sparking like an electric chair.

Then it dawned on me that I had worn the underwear I'd bought in France. It had gold threads woven throughout, and I had liked it because the metallic threads sparkled. It had been an impulse purchase on a different gloomy French day.

"Gosh, I'm sorry." I apologized profusely to the screener, which usually works for me but seemed to annoy him even more. He kept looking at the screen for a pattern. He obviously thought he was about to catch a terrorist red-handed.

His interrogation began with, "How recently did you buy your tickets?" Which was followed by, "What exactly is the reason for your trip? Who is that man with the comb-over accompanying you?" There were other questions I was too perplexed to remember.

When I asked if we were going to miss our flight, he said unsympathetically, "You may never get to go there."

I tried to explain to him about the dress being in fashion, but he was definitely not a fashionista. Next I tried the "I'm just a grandmother going to visit the grandkids" and offered to show him their pictures.

That seemed to annoy him more, his thinking that I thought he was a pushover. The minutes to liftoff were ticking away, and we would almost certainly miss our flight. The gate was the farthest one down the concourse.

The line of people behind me switched to other lanes, or if they had already tubbed their stuff, they drummed their fingers on the edge of the conveyor belt, glancing for the fifth time at their watches, alternated with glares at me.

Mr. Furrowed Inspector, who to his credit was doing his job as diligently as he had been trained to do, still seemed flummoxed by all the lights.

His supervisor who came over, concerned by the delays, looked at the long line and then at me. He must not have thought I looked like a terrorist. He suggested that I make a better choice of outfits and not delay travelers in the future, but he let me through.

"This outfit is going to the Goodwill as soon as I get to Las Vegas. Will we make the flight?" I asked.

"Go ahead," he said gruffly. "I'll call the gate."

I did take the dress to the Goodwill shop the day after we arrived. They told me they loved getting such an up-to-date-dress. I, however, don't miss it, nor I imagine does airport security.

THE HEALER

Every Thanksgiving, it is our tradition to visit Amy in Durham, North Carolina, who through a twist of fate was born on Thanksgiving at 11:00 a.m.

This year, when we arrived at her house, Amy noticed I had a quarter-sized blotch that looked like burnt oatmeal on my face. She insisted I go to her healer, and said it as nonchalantly as if asking me to go to the grocery.

I started sweating and breathing hard. The only healer I'd ever seen was at a Bible revival in Georgia, where under a white tent with bare lightbulbs hanging from the ceiling struts, locals sat in hastily set up folding chairs. The healer held up a snake and spoke in tongues. Not a foreign language, more like gibberish. Then he rolled his eyes back in his head and asked people with afflictions to come forward and be healed. I was six years old and hung back so I wouldn't catch whatever he had.

Amy told me her healer could remove my bump without surgery and it wouldn't come back. Then she ragged on me, suggesting he might fix everything else that was wrong. I knew I didn't have that much time.

I was hesitant to go but was trapped by her suggestion, since I prided myself on my willingness to take risks. I rationalized going would be fine since I could write about the experience, even if the healer's talents didn't work out. Taking a deep breath, I agreed. Before I could change my mind, Amy made me an appointment.

The healer asked her on the phone, "Is your mother open to this idea?"

"Yes, she is," Amy told him, which wasn't exactly the truth.

She and I drove an hour and a half through rolling hills, time enough for me to have second thoughts. Would a healer put me under and forget how to get me out? Would I wander around mumbling words no one else could understand? Would the kids move me to an attic apartment so none of their friends would know insanity ran in the family?

To calm and distract myself, I looked out the window at the passing scenery. That didn't help much. I kept picturing a jangle of bones on a tree beside a double-wide trailer, like the ones we were passing. But when we reached the healer's house, it was brick with an above-ground pool and kids' toys in the backyard.

Thankfully, not the scene I'd dreaded. The man answering the door introduced himself as Jeff. Jeff?

Jeff and I went into a small room with a massage table and a green knitted throw that was starting to unravel at one corner. He had a soothing voice like honey and a kindly smile that could warm the sun. He asked me to lie on the table. We were alone and the lights were low. The world seemed completely still.

Jeff asked me to tell him me if his hands got too hot when he placed them on me. Where would he be placing them? As he did place his hands on different parts of my body, always on top of my hands, his hands became as warm as if he were plugged in.

"Relax and don't forget to breathe."

Easy for him to say.

Jeff told me the growths on my face were an outward sign of inner distress. In pantomime, he unraveled nine threads, pulled out the evil by its roots, and threw the offending threads away.

Next, he placed his hands on top of my hands resting on my belly, his eyes closed, and told me that my stomach was filled with a darkness of problems I'd held in instead of being processed and released. I wondered if he knew I was a Scorpio who held grudges.

He told me he could help me get rid of the murkiness only if I began to let go those things I had repressed.

I was silent, wondering if I could do that after a

lifetime of striving to make life appear to be a Disney story. I finally promised Jeff I'd deal with my angst. I meant it, since I was brought up to keep my word.

Once he said, "Shhh, your spirit animal is talking to me," and I waited impatiently to find out more. All he said was that she was a talkative and upbeat owl.

Then Jeff said something that won my faith: "What is wrong with your left foot?"

How did he know? I hadn't limped or mentioned the bruised heel I'd gotten hiking. He massaged and twisted my foot until suddenly from my knee down I felt better.

Wanting to get my money's worth, I asked him to fix my stiff neck, since my head's turning radius was minuscule. He put his hands on the back of my neck and pressed firmly here and there, then asked me how I felt.

"Light," I said. It was as if my worries and aches had flown away. I felt restored, almost as if I were floating. When I paid his fee, it was with gratitude, my thanks and good-bye to Jeff heartfelt. The lump on my face got smaller and smaller every day for two weeks. Then it was gone. I would probably never know how I came to be healed, but healed I was.

Note: Owl medicine people are associated with clairvoyance. An owl can bring messages in the night through dreams, according to Medicine Cards by Jamie Sams and David Carson.

WHITE GLOVES AND BLUE BOTTLES

Despite rules being unwritten in the South, everyone seemed to follow them precisely. Take, for instance, wearing white gloves. Women wore white gloves for weddings, dances, church, and if they were older, into town. Gloves served to hide the brown-speckled hands of age and make the simplest outfit look special.

Most of the rules we kids followed seemed archaic, and yet we obeyed them as if they were gospel truth. We teenage girls were not allowed to wear slacks or jeans into town or at school. Our unofficial school uniform was a skirt, a blouse with a Peter Pan collar, and saddle oxfords with bobby socks.

We did wear jeans when playing football across our and the neighbor's front yard. Mostly, boys lived around me, but they chose me to kick off the ball, since I kicked it straight, never into the street. And I could only kick it barefoot.

Moms was our family rule maker. Most of her rules centered on the appearance of the yard. She believed that a heavy white wrought-iron bench strategically placed reflected excellent breeding, and that a bottle garden screamed po' trash. This came up when I said I wanted to make a bottle garden. She said no and shook her head for what seemed like the next three days, as a result of the shock.

Bottle gardens (BGs) are best made on newly dead trees. For about an hour a day when the sun shines at the proper angle, colored lights reflect from the bottles and dance on the rocks and flowers. I had thought a BG would look magical alongside the camellias and azaleas in our yard in Auburn.

Years later, after I retired to New Hampshire and was free of constraints, I started working full-time to break every childhood rule I could remember. With the quest for a bottle garden still lurking, I began collecting bottles from friends.

Once, when I was out walking, I saw a huge frosted bottle in a recycling bin ready for pickup in front of a neighbor's house. It said VODKA in raised letters. I looked around to make sure the coast was clear, hoped no one saw me, and snuck the empty bottle away.

Soon my multicolored bottle garden began sprouting at the lake. The review was that it was scraggly. Dick suggested that rather than a ragtag collection, I should concentrate on a big splash of bottles only in shades of blue. But how would I ratchet up my procurement of blue bottles? Buying them from a catalog went against my beliefs. Short of becoming an alcoholic and drinking them empty, I didn't have a clue.

People in really small towns in New Hampshire have to take their recycling and trash to the town dump. When I went there one day and was throwing our separated garbage into the appropriate dumpster, I noticed a summer resident, with his arm back, ready to throw a beautiful blue bottle into the recycling bin, where it would surely shatter. I didn't want to scare the gentle-looking soul, wearing a Polo golf shirt, khaki shorts, and boat shoes without socks, by grabbing his arm and saying "Stop, I need that bottle for my BG." Honestly, I did think briefly about doing it since I was desperate to finish this project. But, as always, I imagined what the newspaper headline might be: Man, accosted at dump by lovely blond woman over a blue bottle, has heart attack. I backed away.

Instead, I went up to my friend Ben, a dump technician, and asked if I could make a contribution to the workers' petty cash fund. They used it for soda or candy from the vending machine. In exchange, they would save me blue bottles for a week.

"Shore," he said.

The next week when I went to the dump there were twenty or thirty bottles in shades of blues stacked helter-skelter in two wire baskets. I was surprised when the same thing happened the week after. Finally, I told Ben, "Y'all can stop now and thanks!"

Back at the lake, visitors' opinions of my BG fall into two camps: one group says, what the heck? The other says, how beautiful. I'll invite the beautiful comment people back next summer for sure.

It is impossible for me to explain my pride, and the liberating feeling I get, when I sit on the rocks with a cup of coffee in the morning, admire the dancing colors and think, at last, it's fini.

At the top of my to-do list is to find Ben at the dump and have him start collecting more blue bottles. You can simply never have enough. What was that splash? Dick jumping off the end of the dock after hearing this?

THE RING

When Moms died in the college football town of Auburn, Alabama, where Janet and Alan and I grew up, she was one hundred years old and a rabid football fan. It was curious that she died on November 8, the day before Janet's and my birthday, three years apart.

The minister came by our house to discuss the funeral, telling us how much everyone in the church loved our mother. "But, uh, I believe the funeral should be on Thursday and not the weekend."

"That's peculiar," I said.

"Ah, you see, this weekend is the big football game, Auburn vs. Georgia. People might make the wrong choice and attend the game instead of the funeral."

"We totally agree," we said, and he sighed and his frown lines disappeared.

At her memorial service on Thursday, the minister

said, "Esther would jump over pews to greet church visitors."

I didn't know about that, but she would push past regulars to make sure newcomers didn't escape. She was eighty then.

Another member at the memorial service mentioned Moms would offer to drive them to church if they missed a few Sundays. "Could she even see over the steering wheel of her Cadillac?" they asked. "We reassured her we would be there on our own, without fail," they said. And they would be.

A third person remembered that at the retirement home, Moms could answer all the trivia questions from college cheerleaders who stopped by to entertain seniors. Moms had a closet full of Auburn University hoodies and T-shirts that she had won answering questions about the football team.

Once when she didn't answer, the students said, "Esther, surely you know this?"

"I do, but I wanted to give someone else a chance."

Then she answered correctly and added another trophy to her growing T-shirt collection.

That night, I realized this would be the last time I'd be in the house where I had studied on the living room rug, and taken the phone with the long cord to the secret place where I used to whisper with my friends.

It would be the last time I'd be in the yard where I'd practiced shooting baskets until I could beat any boy in my class.

It would be the last time I would reflect at the place where Moms had bought me new clothes even when the budget was tight, and given me perfect advice on so many topics.

After the house was cleared out, my daughter Amy, who has intuitive powers, strode into the dining room, rubbed her hand under the shelf of the empty china cupboard, and found a blackened ring.

It looked like there were diamonds in it, and we all thought it was fake.

"Let's get an estimate," Janet and I said, speaking in unison, as we often did when we were little.

"An official appraisal?" Mr. Ware asked, standing in the original jewelry store in our small town.

"No, it may not even be real," we said.

He went to his work area, sprayed cleaner on the ring, and rubbed it with a rag while humming to himself. Was that the Auburn pep song? He took so long that Janet and I, who were chatting about old times, had almost run out of things to say.

Finally, Mr. Ware came up to us. Imitating a magician, he said, "Voilá," stretching open his fingers. There sat a sparkling dinner ring with oodles of gems.

"I declare!" we said together, stunned. I should have worn my sunglasses, I thought.

"It's worth about $9,000," Mr. Ware said.

"Wow! Gosh!" Janet and I said, and then felt like we were on the Antiques Roadshow.

So we three kids—I use that term loosely, although

we will always be kids to each other—decided that whoever took the ring would get $9,000 less from Moms' estate, which was modest.

Initially, only I wanted the ring.

But after dinner, Alan whispered to me, "Janet wants the ring too."

So Janet and I wrote down secret bids which we gave to Alan for safe keeping. We'd all open them after breakfast the next day.

Dick and I went upstairs exhausted from the emotional rollercoaster day.

After we had been asleep for an hour or so, tap, tap, tap sounds filled the room. I thought it must be the same woodpecker I remembered being there in high school, still looking for insects in the tree outside the window. He must be very old by now.

The tapping sounded again. "Em, that's someone knocking," Dick said sleepily. He didn't move. So I crawled out of bed and opened the squeaky door, letting the light from the pine-paneled hallway creep across the rumpled bed. I wanted to always remember how that pine paneling looked at that moment.

Alan was wearing his New Hampshire moose pajamas. "Toots, come out here. It's about the ring."

It was 2:30 a.m. according to my watch.

We crept downstairs, skipping the squeaky third board from the bottom.

Alan said, "I can hear Moms' voice in my head. She wouldn't think it right for only one of you to wear her ring. You and I know you put in the highest bid. How do you think you'll feel when you wear it?"

"Rich?" I said, imagining it on my ring finger.

Alan shook his head.

"Okay, I'll feel bad!"

Alan was right. I probably had put in the highest bid and would feel mean whenever I wore it and Janet couldn't.

"It's late. I'll ask my muse for a solution during the night," I said.

I ask for answers frequently before I go to sleep, but have no idea where they come from.

A couple of hours later, a voice said something to me in my head that sounded like, "Swap ring every year." Nothing else.

A perfect solution. Four-thirty shone from the clock radio.

Next time I'd specify for the answer to arrive after 9:00 a.m., and I laughed—quietly.

In the morning, I put Moms' ring on Janet's finger for her to wear the first year.

It made her look as if she were from old money, sitting in her understated outfit, short curls, and sensible shoes—especially with a $9,000 ring on her finger.

"Don't wear it to the auto repair shop or they will charge you double," I said.

A year later, the first night of the ring switchover, at a birthday dinner at the Magnolia Grill in Durham,

North Carolina, Dick took a picture of the two of us.

"Say ring!" he said. He took a picture of Janet wearing the real ring, and me wearing an off-year fake-diamond ring Amy bought at a department store, so thoughtful to keep things even.

In the photo the real ring sparkles like sunlight dancing on lake water.

But even more brightly in the background you can see a white aura. We kids think it looks exactly like a hundred-year-old woman with a serene smile on her face and no rings on her fingers at all. Moms is still present among us. And that image stays with me to this day.

Moms on her 100th birthday with Emilie, Susan and Isabelle, four generations of women. Each one will wear the ring and pass it down.

WAKE UP AND SMELL THE COFFEE

Sometimes I get annoyed when Dick spends hours watching sports or playing computer bridge. In those moments of pique, I ask myself if he would have been happier staying single. Did he marry me so I could cook and clean, or because he thought I would make a good impression on his firm and friends?

And me, did I marry Dick because he was different from the boys I was raised with in the South in the '50s? Where I came from, girls were expected to be sweet and docile, while Dick encouraged me to be self-sufficient. Was that the reason?

All this second guessing no longer mattered one day in 2012.

Dick was too tired to get out of bed and make the coffee. And his lying there after I got up meant, according to our sharing plan, he would have to make the bed, which was unusual.

That alone should have been an alarm for me, but it wasn't until his heartbeat resembled a Preservation Hall jazz drummer on a riff—thump ta dum, ta da, badda boom—that we headed for the emergency room. His stay at the hospital stretched into five days and as many procedures.

I was afraid my soul mate wouldn't make it through. Whenever I thought that, I'd race into the family waiting room so he couldn't see me cry. Sometimes, I worried he might become an invalid, unable to do the things he loved, and I'd rush into the rest room and weep.

There was an other-worldly feeling when I walked into the house alone at night.

No one for me to ask, "Would you rather have soup and salad, ditto fish and rice?"

No one to answer, "Actually I'd prefer pizza."

No one to throw my arm over when I couldn't sleep, to catch his rhythm and fall back under.

As a coping strategy, I tried to turn my attention to chores, but it didn't really work. I needed to take the car to get the snow tires taken off. Was it May already? I'd forgotten how much I hated waiting in the grungy auto repair office with the stale coffee and ancient magazines about fishing, hunting, and sex. Well, the sex magazines were okay.

Each day I went to Dick's hospital room. It was the size of a large rug, with its adjustable bed, lounge chair, white metal blinds, and gray walls. That didn't matter. We could talk without distractions and Dick was getting better. Mostly, we fell into the comfort of time-tested conversations.

"These rooms could use the cheerful touch of a decorator," I'd say.

"Do you think Tiger will ever make a comeback?" he'd say. We'd laugh.

The hospital let me stay in Dick's room all night if I liked, and when I went home, instead of doing stomach exercises at stoplights, I prayed.

I called the kids and let them know tests and procedures were being done. Two of the girls with ESP said, "I've been feeling sad all weekend."

I found the simplest things became complicated. Although I'd been driving a stick shift and pumping my own gas since I was sixteen, I pulled into the gas station too far from the pump, moved the car closer, got out to pump the gas, the tank wasn't where it had been for the past ten years but had moved to the other side, moved the car, pumped the gas. Whew!

While driving I'd think, Stay focused. Don't hit anyone. It became my new mantra.

I tried to be nice to a revolving door of hospital staff.

"Hello, Heidi," I say to a nurse. "I'm Suzanne," she'd say. "Heidi works on Tuesdays and Thursdays."

When Dick was ready to come home, it was with a pacemaker that would keep his heart beating like a well-oiled clock. Changes would have to be made, but those were things we could deal with.

Together we felt the breezes on the river and saw them dance in the wind, heard the loons' lilting voices, and had the urge to hug the children, their husbands, the grandchildren, and tell them we loved them, without having a reason.

Susan Pearson Spaulding and William McKie Stewart, Jr. are married on
May 20, 1995 in Briarcliff Manor, New York.

Amy Caroline Spaulding and Joseph Michael Tansey, Jr.
are married on June 28, 1997, on Lake Winnipesauke in
Moultonborough, New Hampshire.

On the American River in Lotus, California. Kristiana traveled through a
rapid in her wedding dress, while the unsuspecting groom and guests waited
on September 29, 2007

HAIRSTYLES THAT
CAME AND WENT

Early 1940s: Braids
Janet & Toots Smith

Late 1940s: Toni Perms
Alan, Toots & Janet

1950s: Conservative & Proper
Emilie's Engagement Photo

Late 1960s: Long & Straight
End of the hippie era

1970s: Helmet Head
Dick & Emilie

1980s: Teased & Lots of Hair
Dick, Emilie, Amy, Susie & Kristiana

1990s: Wind Blow & Moussed
Emilie & Dick

2000s: Natural
Emilie, Kristiana, Susan & Amy

EPILOGUE

When I began writing this book, the stories arrived in a hurly-burly way.

I wrote tales about my dad, so the kids and grandkids would know his loving ways.

Then I wove in Southern traditions, like laces intertwining on a shoe. The memories were mostly sweet, except in early days, when I'd have to stop and take a break because I missed my father and it hurt. And I'd pause when Moms' middle child words broke my heart.

A peculiar thing began to happen during the nights. Stories that I didn't remember initially woke me up, seeming to say, Don't forget the time that... This happened so often, instead of trying to remember them till morning, I kept a notebook and pen handy and learned to write in the dark.

While I was shaping the tales of my small-town Georgia days and moving along to life in New York City, I never noticed that writing was shaping me.

It was on one of those early mornings when I crawled out of bed to write—my clear, calm, inspired time of day—that I finally noticed what writing had done. It had given me acceptance. I no longer worried what people thought, or bothered whether my clothes were stylish, or whether my demeanor was of finishing-school quality.

Maybe I had accomplished what I'd set out to do, or maybe not. Regardless, I learned to accept who I am, to find strength from my past, and hope in my future. It is probably what I had been searching for all along. Now I know that being a red-clay girl is being as good as any other, and I'm happy to be just me.

Warm regards,

Emilie Spaulding

www.emiliespaulding.com

ACKNOWLEDGMENTS

Mary Cheever, my first writing teacher, taught our class in the old train station in Sleepy Hollow, New York. In addition to her praise, she said something like this to me, *for goodness sake get a new typewriter ribbon; and did you edit this?* Her honesty made me Teflon tough.

Sharon Elizabeth Wood, my writing teacher in North Carolina is also from the truthfulness school. After being positive to me, she would ask: *where is the arc?* Or she would say: *save that story for your next book* or *this story needs a new close.* Her frank friendship was invaluable.

Henry Louis Gates counseled me as we were separately exiting an airplane in Miami, to use words appropriate to the story's timeline, such as saying colored people, African Americans, or Blacks, depending on the time period.

Bett Barrett worked on every aspect of the book, and helped me find my way. Martha Barrett taught me the importance of having a writing notebook in hand, day and night.

Invaluable readers were Marsha Fillion, Margaret Sofio, Carol Caro, Virginia De Luca, Linda Freeman, Sue Quinlan, Jane Coder, and the New Castle Writing Group led by Priscilla Hodgkins, with Karina Drumheller, Joan Ireland, Dustan Knight, Elaine Nollet, Adele Pulitzer, B.J. Riordan, Mary Robbins, Jenny Rosenson, Claudia Wilbur, and Librarian Christine Collins. Thanks to unflagging encouragement from Betty Tamposi, Nic Robatel, Titia Bozuwa, Pat Spalding, Genevieve Aichele, John Lovering, Amy Antonucci, Steve Kowal, Jon Nash, and Jean Gagne of True Tales radio and the staff of True Tales TV in Portsmouth. Thanks again to my husband and family and sister and brother for their unwavering support. Cover expertise was provided by Nika Dixon, Tom, and Jim Cerny, photographer

Special appreciation goes to Tom Holbrook and Kellsey Metzger of Piscataqua Press at RiverRun Bookstore in Portsmouth, NH, for their creativity, patience, and publishing acumen in producing this my first book, *Red Clay Girl.*

CPSIA information can be obtained
at www.ICGtesting.com
Printed in the USA
BVHW04s1051180518
516408BV00025B/739/P

9 781944 393168